For my Father,
Thank you for passing your love of the outdoors to your sons.

"No one, but he who has partaken thereof, can understand the keen delight of hunting in lonely lands." – Theodore Roosevelt

D0326069

Table of Contents

Purpose

Lets get right to the point. You want to shoot an elk. Perhaps you want a mule deer, antelope, or some other type of western game animal. You didn't open this book up to hear opinions or recollections of fond hunting memories. You simply want to know what you need to do to put an animal on the ground. That's what this book intends to help you with. Hopefully this guide has found its way into the hands of the correct audience, which is the do it yourself (DIY) public land western hunter, or someone who hopes to be. There is certainly more satisfaction in success when it is the result of your own actions, and quite a few pennies to be saved as well. The specific intention of this book is to guide the DIY hunter in making educated hunt *planning* decisions. In addition, this guide should convey the realities and appropriate expectations in hunting the West. With this in mind, I will level with the reader, provide advice, share lessons learned, and burst a few bubbles along the way.

This book is somewhat unique to western hunting literature as it focuses on the planning, preparation, and research that applies to western hunting, before you step foot out of your truck. These are activities you can complete at your home in the off-season. The planning phase of western hunting is as much if not more important than the hunting phase, and treating it as such will multiply your chances of harvesting game. Because no matter how skilled you are as a hunter, if there is no game in your hunting area, you will not be successful. If your hunting area is swarming with other hunters, you will not be successful, and if your perception of the upcoming hunt is in no way close to reality, your hunt will not be rewarding.

The themes covered throughout this text predominantly focus on pursuing rocky mountain elk. Nevertheless, the concepts introduced are consistent with the pursuit of all western big game animals. The book should be used as a guide that one may continuously reference for specific information. Much of the information in this guide is interrelated and therefore isn't always in chronological order given your situation. For that reason, I encourage the reader to finish the whole book before they send out any license or tag applications. As you progress in your western hunting career, many of the topics discussed in this reading should become second nature to you.

This guide is intentionally brief, as it should initiate decision-making, resource gathering and planning. It is written for the perspective of an eastern whitetail deer hunter, as that is the primary hunting group in the US and that is the most interested party in seeking the following knowledge. Even so, the topics presented are useful for hunters of all skill levels seeking western game. Upon completion, the reader will have the intimate knowledge required to plan a western hunt.

Chapter 1 - The Lure of the West

"*Go West, young man, go West. There is health in the country, and room away from our crowds of idlers and imbeciles.*" This resounding advice is attributed to the American Author Horace Greeley in the mid 19th century, the iconic climax of the American West. Although there is some disagreement over who originated the phase "*go West, young man!*" it nevertheless serves as a popular theme to symbolize westward expansion and American Manifest Destiny. As Americans, we hold a romanticized view of the West as being wild and free with endless resources for the taking. Our culture, with substantial influence from the American film industry has created this timeless American West in our minds, and from a good many perspectives it still exists. There are still rugged snowcapped mountains, gigantic tracts of backcountry, fierce creatures, chilling blizzards, and countless dangers for those who venture into the wilderness. The opportunities for an outdoorsman are endless. If you couple these ideas with the amount of public land available, you can spend a lifetime exploring and hunting and still only cover a fraction of the western landscape. As hunters, we have an innate drive to seek out and harness this majestic and unflinching wilderness. It's the lure of the West; it will bring you here and keep you coming back!

Tenmile Range, Colorado

Upon arrival in the western US, the first thing many notice is the expansiveness of the country. From the mountains and open spaces to the animals that call it home, everything seems much bigger than the eastern US. The population of the Rocky Mountains is a mere fragment of the rest of the country. With undeveloped land everywhere, the sporting challenges are boundless for a hunter, no matter what flavor you prefer. Where are you going for opening day of rifle season? Well, that depends on what animal species you are asking about. Whitetail deer are not the only big game in town. Each year in many western states you can easily hunt elk, deer, antelope, and bear. There are also sheep, goat, moose, and multiple other species and subspecies, although tags can be a bit harder to draw for these.

These are some of the ideas and dreams that brought me to Colorado years ago. Upon arrival, I naively assumed elk hunting would be as easy to pick up as eastern whitetail hunting. I quickly learned that the similarities are few and the differences are many. Hunting over small food plots, in tree-stands, on small parcels of land, or close to roads are strategies that simply do not bear fruit. Back East, one can assume that most stretches of undeveloped woods hold deer; this is not the case out West. With the over abundance of vacant land, the game has choices. In short, hunting public land in the West is much harder than private land deer hunting back East. You're not hunting the back 40 anymore. Simply put, whitetail tactics usually do not apply and usually will not work.

The inspiration for writing this book comes from personal experience. By that I mean numerous personal blunders that slowly led to continued success. It also comes from continuously meeting unsuccessful first time hunters that are very reminiscent of my initial years in the Rockies. Year after year thousands of eastern hunters descend on the Rockies with dreams of giant bucks and bulls. These dreams are born by television shows, hunting articles, second hand stories, and product advertisements. Most inexperienced hunters assume that western hunting is similar to eastern hunting, and their tactics will prevail based on their eastern experiences and determination. Don't fall victim to this misunderstanding. The reality is: hunting western game is worlds apart from hunting eastern whitetails.

Nonetheless, aspiring hunters should not fret a dismal outcome. This guide describes many strategies that will substantially increase your odds of making a kill. Many western hunts do end in success, it just takes a level of planning and knowledge that veterans keep to themselves and the beginner has difficulty uncovering. Without a doubt, boots on the ground experience in western hunting is one of the best methods to improve your chances of success. However, the beginner does not have this weapon in their arsenal. They must begin with information gathering. All successful western hunts begin with tag research, tag applications, specific hunting area research, and thoughtful planning. Hunt execution is only the final step. Let's discuss what you should be learning first, the lay of the land and the animals that inhabit it.

Chapter 2 - Western Terrain

Imagine you are traveling West across the United States from the Virginia coast. As you start your journey, you leave the coastline and pass through numerous small towns and large cities. Dwellings speckle the countryside and it is difficult to travel very far without being in view of homes and businesses. Outside of the metropolitan areas, much of the passing countryside is rich agricultural farmland separated by small patches of forest. The land steadily rises and as you continue over rolling hills and lazy rivers and begin to ascend the Appalachian Mountains. Soon the checkerboard of deciduous forest and farmland begins to include steep hills and mountain ridges. You continue heading West and after breaching the Appalachian Mountain passes you begin to slowly descend into the Mississippi River Valley. The climate through this entire region is quite similar with only slight variations in humidity and temperature as you fluctuate in elevation. Much of the eastern United States encompasses a similar ecosystem and terrain. The Appalachian Mountains offered the only substantial elevation change on your journey, but even these were not so formidable. Continuing on your westward journey, you cross the Mississippi River and slowly begin to gain elevation. As you climb from the lowlands, you gradually notice a few changes. The air begins to lose its humidity. The trees become sparse. The towns and cities that dotted the countryside are more spread apart and generally smaller in size. Heading further West, you increasingly notice the disappearance of trees altogether with the only reminiscence being those you find next to bodies of water. The land has also become exceptionally flat. You have now entered what was once dubbed "the great American desert," and what we now simply refer to as "the plains." The plains stretch continuously through many states, only to be broken by vastly separated rivers and small hills. Rivers reside in canyons that wind upward into the plains through coulees. There is a clear lack of foliage and the land of the whitetail deer is replaced with the land of the pronghorn and mule deer. Steadily pushing further West, the terrain continues upward with little to no deviation in the barren landscape. The plains seem endless. You can imagine how waves of buffalo once blanketed the land by the thousands. As you recount the days of cowboys and Indians, you begin to notice a faint floating horizon in the distance. As you draw closer, the ominous mirage begins to take form. The angry spine of plate tectonics grows higher and higher. The jagged peaks of the snowcapped Rocky Mountains paint the perfect western landscape. You have now reached elk country.

The Rocky Mountains range from Alaska to Mexico, and are as diverse as they are long. One can only imagine what went through the minds of explorers and pioneers the first time they set eyes on the Rocky Mountains. Early settlers had never encountered such a forbidding landscape, and many contemporary hunters never have either. Western hunting terrain is not homogenous. The Rockies rise out of the plains and crest in snowcapped peaks high above tree line. They are separated by deep valleys and canyons only to rise and fall into rocky bluffs again and again. Other breaks in the mountain spine sometimes drop into flat plains similar to those on the eastern edge of the Rockies. In some regions the precipitous elevation drops into arid desert terrain. The arid terrain forms unique rock formations and canyon systems quickly replaced by forested slopes as the land rises in elevation once again. The Rockies vary in size and shape from one range to the next.

The majority of the Rockies reside in 12 western states. Each state has multiple ranges, all with unique characteristics and terrain (with the exception of South Dakota, which only has one range). The habitat, ecosystem, and foliage vary greatly all dependent on one main factor: elevation.

Alpine Tundra, Colorado

In general, elevation dictates the ecosystem present in the Rockies. Lower elevations tend to receive less precipitation than higher elevations. Less precipitation equals less vegetation. The amount of moisture also greatly dictates what type of vegetation is present. Grass grows with minimal moisture. Coniferous trees require additional levels of moisture, and deciduous vegetation requires more moisture than coniferous. Rising from the low-lying canyons, arid desert-like terrain turns into monotonous grassland. Grasslands wind upward through valleys and rise into coniferous montane forest. Deciduous plants and trees exist only in moist drainages or next to bodies of water. Only the broadleaf aspen tree shares in the expansive tracts of dominating coniferous forest. Coniferous forest is made up of many tree species, all of which carve out a specific niche habitat. As you rise in elevation and precipitation levels, some of the common conifers you will find are pinion, juniper, ponderosa, spruce, lodgepole, and fir. Continue rising and the trees become smaller and smaller. The small stunted coniferous trees distinguish the subalpine forest, which continues to the point known as tree line. Tree line is the high elevation upward edge of the forest. The Rockies rise higher in elevation than trees can survive, and the habitat above tree line is referred to as alpine tundra. Grasses, shale, and rocky peaks characterize the alpine tundra. Although the climate at this elevation is harsh, the grasses during summer months can be quite attractive to wild game, and the majestic peaks are also quite attractive to outdoor enthusiasts. All of these ecosystems may not be present in a given area, as it takes many thousand feet in elevation gain to rise from an arid canyon to a soaring alpine peak. The contrast of these ecosystems is also more apparent in certain regions. For instance, one could easily depict all ecosystems looking at Utah's La Sal Mountains from Arches National Park, but you would be hard pressed to find desert terrain anywhere near Montana's Glacier National Park. The further South you go in the Rockies, the more arid desert habitat you will find. The further North you go, the less arid and moister habitat you will find.

Glacier National Park, Montana

The Southwestern United States has very high sun intensity. This intensity lessens as you travel North and East. For this reason, the Southwestern Rockies are more arid than their neighbors to the North and East, and so are the valleys in between them. The slopes in the Rockies that face South and West also receive much more direct sunlight due to their positioning in relation to the sun. More direct sunlight creates drier terrain and less moisture dictates less vegetation. Many South and West facing slopes in the Rockies are void of trees due to the sun intensity on these slopes. At higher elevations, the additional precipitation outweighs the sun intensity and South and West facing slopes become forested. Flat mountain valleys are also subject to a treeless phenomenon. Thus many flat valleys are long and narrow grassy meadows. In contrast, North and East facing slopes hold more moisture as they receive less debilitating sunlight. This means they often are lush and densely vegetated. They also remain this way longer as the summer heat dries out the landscape. As you may have guessed, the game uses the terrain characteristics to their benefit given the time of year, food present, and cover needed.

La Sal Mountains, Utah

The primary hunting terrain for western hunters is on public land. This is because access is granted free of charge to the general public. Private land can be very good hunting terrain as well, but access is not granted without permission and permission usually requires some type of fee or landowner relationship. The good news is that the majority of prime elk and mule deer terrain is actually located on public land, and there is a lot of it across the West. US public land comes in many shapes, forms, and sizes. Some examples include National Forests, Bureau of Land Management Properties (BLM), National Parks, National Wildlife Refuges, State Parks, State Forests, County Parks, and various other public access areas. Many states also promote private land access through various public programs distinct to each state. Public land properties are managed by separate governing bodies and have different primary uses. The land uses are established by each specific governing body and sometimes differ by specific site location. Across the West, the majority of hunting terrain is on National Forest and BLM land. The Forest Service (USFS) division of the US Department of Agriculture manages all of the National Forests. As the name suggests, USFS land is primarily forested mountain terrain. The United States boasts 155 different National Forests covering around 193 million acres.[i] Remarkably, almost 90% of this land lies West of the Mississippi River, mostly in the Rocky Mountain region. The Department of the Interior, Bureau of Land Management, governs all of the BLM land. While USFS land is mostly forested, BLM land covers many different types of terrain. BLM land encompasses roughly 245 million acres, located primarily in 12 western states.[ii] To give some perspective, in Colorado alone, there are over 23 million acres of National Forest and BLM land.[iii] Eastern public land hunting is often crowded due to land size compared to human population. As you can see from the approximate acreage, there is a bit more elbowroom in the West.

The general colonization of our country spread from East to West, and the concept of public land preservation came long after colonization. For this simple reason, most of the preserved public land in our country resides in the western states. As the pioneers moved West to homestead, they logically chose areas to settle for agriculture, natural resources, accessibility, and climate. In the Rockies, these areas tend to be the easier to access lower elevation mountain valleys, open spaces, and river corridors. The land that remained was mostly inhospitable mountain forest, arid regions, and areas located far off the beaten path. As the conservation movement gained momentum in the early twentieth century, these unoccupied areas quickly became preserved as public land.

In many instances, you have varying types of land adjacent to one another. This creates a checkerboard of diverse public and private lands. Mountains separated by open valleys are characterized by National Forests separated by private ranches. The access to the National Forest may consist of only a few USFS roads, with the far edges of the public land only reachable by foot or horseback. As public boundaries often adjoin private land, it is the responsibility of the hunter to be aware of land boundaries and rules within that area. Nearly all site-specific regulations are posted at public land access points and usually online as well. Simply read the signs as you enter or look up the rules online beforehand. Fortunately for hunters, the two main bodies of public land (National Forest and BLM) are receptive to sportsmen and outdoor enthusiasts. Some examples of more specific regulations that may come into play are camping restrictions, mode of travel permitted (e.g. ATV, mountain bike, horses, etc.), and seasonal closures. All areas are monitored for illegal activity by various positions of authority. Failure to comply with regulations will eventually ensure an unpleasant experience with the authorities.

Elk hunting is a popular activity. As access to public land is granted to all who please, you will encounter other hunters in the field. Even though there is plentiful public land across the West, some areas have intense hunter competition and overcrowding issues. This is often due to a specific area's ease of access. Large tracts of public land are often bordered by private land that funnels public land entry to a few specific locations. For example, in a fifty square mile block of National Forest, there may only be public access every ten miles or so. Access comes in the form of USFS roads, trailheads, parking areas, and usually is permitted anywhere where public land meets a public road. Some USFS roads are in good condition, and others are not. Some are closer to cities and towns than others. Some access areas are flat while others are in sheer mountains. For these reasons, hunters cluster around the areas with close access, maintained roads, open meadows, and easier hiking. This bears repeating: beware of hunting areas that are close to metropolitan areas, close to main roads, on flat and easy hiking ground, in wide open valleys and meadows, and ones that are tourist destinations. Any area that is overly easy to access is susceptible to overcrowding. Regardless, there is often so much public land in a general area that you can easily separate yourself from other hunters if you avoid these attributes and complete a little research, planning, and legwork.

Sawatch Range, Colorado

Hopefully this has painted a brief picture of the rocky mountain terrain and animal habitat. In summary, arid regions wind upward into grassy plains, mountain valleys and open meadows. These meadows transition into sloping mountain forests covered by coniferous trees and occasional aspen breaks. North and East facing slopes are densely vegetated while South and West facing slopes are more open. As you travel higher in elevation, the forests dwindle into the open grasslands of the alpine tundra. If the land continues to rise, the alpine tundra leads into rocky outcroppings and jagged peaks. Some or all of these habitats may be present in a specific area, dominated by the specific geographic and elevation features. All of these ecosystems hold western game in some form or another. Each habitat appeals to each species for different reasons and during different times of the year. The Rockies are painted with public land, most of which is either National Forest or BLM land. Usage of public land varies from location to location, and its popularity tends to rise with proximity and ease of access.

Chapter 3 - Elk Behavior

After giving an overview of western terrain it's appropriate that an explanation be given of how elk use it. Elk behave differently during different periods of the year. As habitual information concerns the general locations of elk, it should have a strong bearing on your decisions regarding a potential hunt. With the focus of this book on hunt planning, this chapter focuses on game tendencies during the hunting seasons.

The journals of Lewis and Clark characterize elk as meadow dwelling creatures that roam the open spaces of our western landscape in large herds. In those days, elk predominantly inhabited the plains and mountain valleys. If you vacation to Yellowstone National Park, this is still where you will find them. If you attempt to find them in the plains and valleys on our public hunting lands, you may only find yourself confused. Over the last two hundred years, elk have changed addresses. Due to loss of habitat, human pressure, and reasons too numerous to list, elk now primarily inhabit the forested slopes of our mountains. Their once expansive range largely disappeared from the East, Mid-west, and plains. Lucky for hunters, the early 1900's ushered in a new way of thinking. Waves of sustainable wildlife management have done well to preserve our land and game animals. Regulated hunting seasons and wildlife reintroduction efforts returned large elk populations across the western states and provinces. Efforts have now even established sustainable elk herds in multiple eastern states and provinces. But modern elk do not behave in the same manner as their plain dwelling relatives did. Most of our open plains regions have since been fenced and divided into farms and ranches. On the contrary, much of our mountainous regions have been preserved. Seizing the unaltered mountain land and utilizing the safety of the forest, elk have become residents of the rugged Rocky Mountains. But even though elk have relocated their primary habitat, they haven't forgotten all of their original tendencies and still carry some of the characteristics of plains game.

The previous chapter gave descriptions of a vast and varied Rocky Mountain region. Because the land is so vast and varied, it favors the nomadic wanderer. Given the contrasting ecosystems, elk utilize the different terrain for its greater benefit during different times of the year. Some elk, commonly referred to as resident elk, live within smaller ranges and do not migrate each year. This is because some areas provide all the needed habitat characteristics an elk desires as well as a suitable climate. Resident elk movement patterns are within a much smaller area, but even though they live in a smaller area they still posses an uncanny wandering characteristic. However the majority of elk do migrate, at least to some extent, and their behavioral patterns vary for other reasons as well. Thus we will focus our discussions on migratory elk, as resident elk are much fewer in number. In the next paragraph we will examine what causes elk movement patterns in the context of the annual hunting seasons.

Due to the nature of elk and the timing of elk hunting seasons, there are general benefits in hunting each time of the year. Let's begin with the warmer months. This is when elk inhabit what is referred to as their summer range. During the summer, food is abundant and elk seek out leisure feeding areas. Elk also try to avoid the summer heat and swarming bugs. Coincidentally, this is a very pleasant time of year to feed on the grasses in the highly elevated mountain parks and forests and even the open meadows above tree line. Elk will begin to move up into their summer range when snow and cold weather recedes in the spring. They will remain in these elevated areas through the warmer months, usually until early fall when the bulls begin to feel the testosterone rumblings of the breeding season. State by state archery seasons usually begin from late August to early September. Elk will still be in their summer range when archery seasons begin. Feeding is the dominant factor in elk behavior this time of year. Early archery season and pre-rut hunting takes place at the highest of elevations and by patterning elk feeding habits. In general, elk establish both a bedding area and a feeding area and repetitively travel between each on a daily basis. They travel to feed in the evenings, remain in feeding areas overnight, and travel back to the bedding grounds in the morning. If not pressured, they tend use the same travel routes and trails quite routinely. Elk are commonly referred to as grazers, rather than browsers. This means they primarily eat grasses and forbs directly growing from the ground. They also prefer to feed in open areas, as this is the best place to find those food sources. Open feeding areas typically occur above tree line, on South or West facing slopes, or in mountain meadows. Any secluded grassy area is attractive to an elk. Public land elk typically begin travelling to feeding areas well before sunset, but often will not leave the safety of the forest until dusk. Likewise, they begin their daily journey back to their bedding areas as dawn arrives. The likelihood of elk spending daylight hours in open areas is usually dependent on the amount of pressure in a given area. More pressure equals less daylight hours spent in the open. Elk bedding areas are often higher in elevation than feeding areas, except if they are feeding above tree line. Thus they commonly travel down to feed and up to bed. They prefer to bed in areas with good cover, which is often North and East facing steep slopes. They also favor bedding on mountain benches. Elk bed facing downhill and monitor the wind while peering into the areas below them. Intercepting elk traveling to and from feeding and bedding areas or simply at the feeding area is the prime hunting tactic this time of year.

Bull Elk Feeding in Meadow, Colorado

As September rolls on, elk begin to focus on another instinctual drive: breeding. The peak in breeding activity is usually localized, but the majority of elk are rutting by mid-September. September is also when bulls begin to bugle. The benefits of hunting any rutting animal are immense; however the elk bugle is a unique phenomenon. The greatest benefit is that it announces a bulls' position from a distance. Hunting the elk rut is a fantastic time to be in the woods. Calling elk this time of year is also a huge benefit to any hunter. Similar to whitetail deer, the intensity of the rut will last a few weeks. As the rut kicks in, the elk will stay within their summer range but tend to drop down slightly in elevation. This means they will primarily inhabit the sloping montane forests below the tree line and subalpine forests. Breeding becomes their main behavioral factor, especially for the bulls. The bulls herd harems of cows together like a dog to sheep and eject all less dominant bulls from the herd. The term harem is used to denote a collection of cows grouped together by a bull for breeding purposes. Dominant bulls round up as many cows into their harem as they can and attempt to breed each one. Elk are very aggressive creatures during the breeding season, and very vocal as well. Dominant bulls will constantly ward off challenging bulls and attempt to maintain and grow their harem. The inferior, or satellite bulls, follow the herds at a distance or roam the mountainside looking for open breeding invitations. The benefit to hunting this time of year is that you are pursuing unpressured rut crazed vocal bulls while sharing the woods with less people. Unpressured because archery seasons typically take place before rifle seasons and less people tend to bow hunt than rifle hunt. The more elk get hunted, the more they get educated, and the more elusive they become. In the initial hunting seasons, elk are much less spooky, closer to the public land access points, and easier to locate. Many states also include muzzleloader seasons during this time of year. The elk herds will still consistently travel between feeding and bedding areas, and the bulls announce their location along the way. The satellite bulls travel outside of the herds as they search for cows and challenge other bulls for breeding rights. Herds range in size and number. Some areas may have only a few large herds, while others have many smaller herds. In any case, you can usually bet that there is a bull in close proximity to any group of cows this time of year. The primary hunting tactic during the rut is to locate elk through their bugles. You can then either attempt to call them in range by impersonating cows or challenging bulls, or simply try to intercept them on their travel route. Another tactic this time of year is to search out bull wallows and stand hunt over them. We will further discuss bull wallows in the scouting section of this book. As the height of the rut passes, the weather cools and autumn sets in. The breeding drive slowly tapers off and bulls transition to energy recovery behavior and concentrate on feeding again.

On a state-by-state basis, initial rifle seasons typically begin in October and run through November. If rifle seasons open in the very beginning of October you may catch the tail end of the rut. This can be a great benefit as elk are more vulnerable and hunters can shoot from longer distances. As the month of October progresses, elk steadily resume the bedding and feeding behavioral pattern usually near their recent rutting areas. Hunters should base their strategy on this behavior for unpressured elk this time of year. Locate the feeding and bedding areas and keep an ear open for bugles and late rutting activity. If the elk do not seem to be rutting, focus solely on feeding areas and travel routes. If still rutting, follow the bugles and try your hand at calling.

Notice I mentioned that you should use these strategies for *unpressured* elk. Rifle seasons throw the biggest and most unpredictable curveball into the mix. This curveball is the hunters themselves. In many ways, other hunters are your largest obstacle in public land hunting, especially so in the rifle seasons. Not only do you need to find elk, but you also need to avoid other hunters. That's what the elk will be doing as well. There is a strong correlation with the amount of elk you see and the absence of hunters in your area. Elk quickly leave town when they are pressured. Leaving town is not much of an exaggeration either; pressured elk will often travel miles away. This tendency is frequently attributed to their days on the plains. Plains game does not have the luxury of cover, so they use distance to protect themselves from danger. Elk do the same. Because pressured elk are so difficult to hunt, savvy hunters seek limited tag units and lesser-known hunting areas.

Cow Elk Feeding in Meadow, Colorado

Overcrowding in certain areas and during specific hunting seasons is rampant in public land elk hunting, and elk seem to know this better than hunters do. As you can imagine, the behavioral pattern that pressured elk follow is the complete avoidance of hunters. Hunters need to critically consider this factor when planning a hunt for pressured elk. One can assume a given area is pressured after a few days of the first rifle season, unless the tags are highly limited. This bears repeating: if you are hunting general rifle seasons, your elk will be pressured after a few days. Elk completely leave pressured areas and congregate in remote areas and on private land. If hunting pressured elk, target refuge areas and travel corridors such as saddles and escape routes. Pressured elk movement is generally into large herds and down in elevation.

Lower elevations typically are private land. An easy method to avoid this pressured elk dilemma is to hunt at the beginning of the rifle season or in the earlier seasons. Many states offer multiple rifle seasons. If you are looking for a bull, the earlier the season, the better your chances are of avoiding pressure.

As October and November wear on, the weather continues to change and winter tightens its grip on the high country. For western game, this often necessitates a migration to greener pastures. Many states continue their rifle seasons in this time of year. The general elk migration movement is to areas that have a milder climate, which are ultimately areas that are lower in elevation. Migrations occur across the West and vary in timing and distance. Movement due to hunting pressure also spurs migrations to new territory. Even so, migration timing is usually dependent upon local weather. If the snows and temperatures drop earlier in the fall, the elk will migrate earlier. Hard to believe, but the commonly accepted amount of snow to get elk moving is about 18 inches. Distance of travel depends on their habitual wintering grounds. Elk return to the same winter areas year after year. If their wintering grounds are in close proximity, the migration distance will not be far. On the other end of the spectrum, collared elk have been tracked traveling dozens of miles to habitual wintering grounds. Man-made obstacles such as interstates and neighborhoods often interrupt traditional migration routes. Elk either travel around such obstacles or abandon the migration route altogether. Many hunters each year seek out routine migration corridors to hunt travelling elk. This is feast or famine style of hunting as elk move through the hinterlands between their summer and winter ranges. If you can pinpoint a migration zone, you can hit a bonanza. If targeting a migration zone, look for natural pinch points in the geography, such as saddles and ridgelines. Heavily used trails can also show signs of migration. Hunters often locate such areas through scouting, past experience, or tips. The main hunting tactic is to stand hunt over natural concentration zones and hope the elk move through while on stand. As this period overlaps with rifle seasons, always bear in mind the hunting pressure factor. The migration is complete when elk arrive at their winter range.

Winter ranges are lower in elevation and have much milder winter climates than summer ranges. These are your low mountain valleys, plains regions, and mountain foothills. The elk have travelled here to avoid the harsh weather. During this time period, elk often inhabit open terrain in large herds. Once again, many states hold rifle seasons this time of year. Hunting can be boom or bust once more, as the animals may only be in a few large groups. Elk can be quite vulnerable in the open spaces and often winter ranges overlap large private ranches. For that reason, private land access is exceptionally beneficial this time of year. Many state agencies take advantage of this time period by increasing or decreasing the number of cow tags issued in an effort to reach herd population objectives. If elk winter ranges do happen to be on public land, this is a good time to be out in the field. Hunters should target traditional winter ranges and spend the majority of their time glassing and searching for the herds. This may include covering long distances by vehicle and foot. Hunting usually requires open terrain stalking and long distance shooting. A couple drawbacks in hunting this season are damaged antlers and the fact that many bulls have already been harvested. The quality of the elk's winter range is often the most significant factor on general herd size and health. During winter, elk are at their weakest. Herds can only grow to a size that their winter range can support. If elk cannot access ample winter range, they will not grow into large herds no matter how plentiful the adjacent summer range is. Extreme winters can have detrimental effects on elk herds. Each year state biologists track the rise and fall of elk populations due to winter weather conditions. Herds can take many years to rebound after an extremely harsh winter. Sadly, many traditional wintering grounds are now inhabited by human settlement. Loss of habitat is the central reason elk may never reach their historical populations. Most hunting seasons end at some point during the winter months. The game tends to wait out the winter on these ranges and as the weather warms they begin the cycle of the next year.

Elk on Winter Range, Colorado

If you have not witnessed elk habitat or behavior firsthand, this abstract information may be somewhat hard to digest. To gain more perspective on elk behavior, we can make a few comparisons to whitetail deer.

Whitetail deer can be described as secretive and habitual creatures with small home ranges, often living their entire lives in a an area of around 640 acres.[iv] In contrast, elk are nomadic creatures that live in vast tracts of land with home ranges anywhere from 2,500 to 10,000 acres.[v] Those that migrate long distances can have even larger ranges. Whitetail population densities are known to range beyond 50 deer per square mile in many areas of the United States. High population densities for elk are often estimated just above 5 elk per square mile. Less game, in larger areas, with nomadic tendencies, makes the hunting situation quite different. When elk do decide to employ their nomadic tendencies, they move miles away; a seemingly useful plains game technique that has yet to diminish. You can count on a very spooked whitetail deer to run a few hundred yards. You can count on a very spooked elk to go at least a mile. In fact, elk often leave the general area when spooked. That means if you spook an elk, his bedding and feeding pattern is going to change and he will not show back up where you spooked him. Depending on how pressured they are or what time of year it is, they may vacate the area until the next year. It's a hard pill to swallow, but if you scare an elk, he is a likely a goner until next season. This can really throw a boomerang into public land hunting. While pressured whitetails often go nocturnal or hide out in thickets, elk herds vacate entire areas. It is hard to imagine that hundreds of elk will completely disappear from giant tracts of forest, but it happens every year. Hunters will move in, and elk will completely move out. Western hunters cover large areas when they hunt. Hunting techniques such as stalking, glassing, tracking, calling, and still-hunting pressure areas much more than stand hunting. That means it doesn't take too many hunters to pressure a large area. Elk also do not intermingle with human existence as whitetails do. All over the United States you commonly find whitetails in urban corridors living in very close proximity to people. This does exist to some extent with elk, but usually only in areas where they are not hunted. Elk tend to keep their distance from homes and human dwellings. Their human comfort distance is much further than deer, if they have one at all. Usually you simply don't see elk where humans frequent.

During rutting periods elk behavior is quite exceptional, especially so for bulls. Whereas whitetails implement a mate and move on strategy, bull elk herd cows together then stand guard over them. They then guard these harems of cows and attempt to breed each cow in the harem. Less dominant bulls will watch and follow at a distance. Some may challenge a herd bull, others may try to sneak off with cows or breed those that stray from the main herd. In any case, the elk harem technique is quite different than the mate and move on whitetail technique.

Many of these characteristics present a sense of difficulty in western hunting, but there is a silver lining. For instance, because elk are constantly wandering, they are not as intimate with their surroundings as whitetails are. That means they are slower to notice oddly shaped human figures in the woods. They also aren't as nervous or wary as whitetails are. Hunters typically do not try to stalk whitetails, their senses are too keen and they spook too easily. This is not the case with elk and other western game. Hunters with all weapon types successfully stalk and harvest elk every year. Minor noises usually do not spook them, your appearance doesn't seem to be as distinguishable, and they hesitate when they do see you. That's right; elk do not immediately bolt when they sense something is wrong. Elk are social creatures. They tend to live in herds of varying sizes. The herds are largest during the rut, when pressured, and during the late winter months. Herds typically have a dominant cow that calls the shots of where to go and when to move. This is commonly referred to as the lead cow. If elk in a group detect your presence, the spooked elk will wait until the lead cow decides to leave before they follow. Elk that sense danger will usually mill around and act alarmed, but delay running until the lead cow decides its time to go. If you find yourself in this position, you can use the little time you have to take action. In addition, scared elk will often stop running if you send out a cow call. Being social creatures, they believe they may have mistaken danger for another elk. A quick call may delay the elk leaving, but usually only long enough to notice that there isn't another elk standing there. Nonetheless, it may buy you enough time for a shot. If an elk is alone it will move on its own accord, as there is no lead cow to call the shots. There is also no delay if you are very close to a herd or very boisterous in how you spook them. As far as the herds and lead cows go, it may take elk a few moments to get moving but when they decide to get going don't expect them to stop anytime soon.

White-tailed Deer, Montana

While their eyes and ears don't seem to be quite as fearful as a whitetail's, beware of their nose. If elk smell you, they are gone, plain and simple. No tricks, camouflage, or calls will help you here. Elk live in areas with little to no trace of human scent. That means even the smallest whiff will send them to the next county. You can also count on the tumultuous terrain in elk country to keep the wind swirling. Rocky Mountain breezes are somewhat steady in the morning and evening, but the wind in the middle of the day doesn't abide by any rules. Bear in mind your thermals as well. Thermals rise and fall with the temperature, often up in the morning and down in the evening, and they carry your scent with them. Scent control clothing, soap and cover scent assists in masking human odor, but the physical activity involved in traversing elk terrain tends to keep you sweating and disbursing human scent.

The vocal nature of elk is also a positive difference. Whitetail deer have very few notable calls. Outside of the rut, these deer rarely make social noises useful for hunters. On the other hand, elk are very social creatures that are constantly communicating all year long. A bull bugle can be heard from one ridge to the next, and herds constantly chirp and mew to one another for a multitude of reasons. Hunters often hear elk long before they see them. Not to mention that calling is one of the most popular tactics in hunting elk.

There is also the obvious size difference. Bull elk may weigh anywhere from 500 to 1,000 pounds. Deer are significantly smaller. What does this mean? Elk have more body mass, more blood, and better success at surviving improperly placed shots. They make much more noise when walking and running, and a lot more when crashing. This also means the meat is much more difficult to transport to your vehicle, and your harvest is frequently a long distance from your car. You can count on having a good bit of work to do if you are successful. This is often overlooked by novice western hunters, but should be seriously considered when planning a hunt deep in the backcountry.

Hopefully this chapter has helped to illustrate the how elk utilize the terrain they inhabit. Our discussions involved their movements during the different seasons, the timing of the hunting seasons, and common hunting tactics employed based on their behavior. We also discussed a few comparisons to whitetail deer to gain perspective on the species differences. With these ideas in mind, next we will explore the expectations a hunter should have when making decisions for a hunt.

Chapter 4 - Expectations

Make no mistake; elk hunting can be one of the most exhilarating hunting experiences of your life. Elk are no doubt the king of the antlered beasts in North America. No other animal possesses such impressive headgear or exhibits such rutting insanity. They also offer exceptional table fare and a wilderness experience unique to eastern hunting. However, elk hunting can also be some of the slowest and most aggravating hunting you have ever experienced. The tendencies of elk and the terrain they inhabit certainly give elk the upper hand, and their pursuers, no matter how diligent, will succumb to failure more than success.

Here comes the first bubble burst. As a self-guided elk hunter, do not expect to replicate what you have seen on the outdoor channel. This bears repeating, hunting as seen on television is not the realistic hunting experience you will encounter in the field. This is especially true for the self-guided hunter on public land. Most hunting shows are filmed on guided hunts and/or on private land. A guide does all the homework for the hunter, with a price tag. Private land restricts hunter access and controls the amount of hunting pressure in a given area. You probably cannot devote the amount of time to hunting that a guide does, and you likely don't have access to large private hunting ranches. Therefore, you will not replicate what you have seen on television, plain and simple. You also don't see many episodes where the hunters don't see any game or encounter hunter overcrowding. That's because only exciting footage makes it to the screen. Maybe you have five minutes of television worthy action in a full week of hunting. If you want to replicate what you have seen on TV, you are going to need to shell out some cash for an outfitter or access some private land to do so. To have a successful self-guided hunt, you save the money, but you will need to do your homework and research. After doing your research, you may then find success, but likely not to the degree of our television stars.

To get the most enjoyment out of your hunt, the best way to begin is by coming to terms with a few facts and managing your expectations. If you have high expectations and do not see many elk, you may find yourself confused and let down. If you had known your hunting area's potential beforehand, you may not feel so let down. If you factually know that you are going to an area that has consistently produced large bulls, you can reasonably set your expectations at this level. Simply put, before you go elk hunting, you need to gauge your expectations according to where you will be hunting.

Here comes the next bubble burst. Truth be told, elk hunting success rates are low. Bull success rates are even lower, and mature bull success rates are even lower than that. Across the West, you can expect overall either sex elk harvest rates to linger somewhere around 20%. Cut that in half for bulls, and in half again for mature bulls. This means that four out of five hunters return home empty handed every year; however we all know that some hunters are successful almost every year. This is not a phenomenon specific to elk hunting. No matter what the quarry is, some hunters harvest every year, while other hunters are not so lucky. The not so lucky hunters tend to be beginners or those hunting less favorable property. Now, we all would like to consider ourselves the veteran who bags nearly every year, but the truth is most of us are not. If you are hunting the West for the first time, you are a beginner and you may be hunting less than favorable property. Just like that, the odds are now against you. You should also keep in mind that many elk seasons are shorter than whitetail seasons. For instance, many whitetail archery seasons span three to five months. Some of the longest elk archery seasons span about one month. In addition, non-resident elk hunts are usually conducted within a short vacation time period. You may bag whitetails every year, but if you only had one week to hunt whitetails, would you be so successful?

As with most statistics, we need to read between the lines. A 20% success rate is an average, meaning some areas have lower success rates and others have higher, much higher. So obviously hunters should target areas with proven high success rates and avoid the opposite. Along with targeting specific hunting areas there are many other ways to increase or decrease your personal success rate. And the best part is, many of the techniques are easy and the resources are available at your fingertips.

Before going any further, let's get down to basics and touch on one of the main themes of this book. The following concept is simple, but it can be a hard pill to swallow. It will help level your expectations with reality, increase your odds in harvesting, and provide you with a quality experience more so than any other aspect of western hunting:

Your personal hunting success is a direct result of the potential of where you are hunting. If elk trophy potential or elk populations are not great in your hunting area, don't expect to see large bulls or many elk.

It does matter how skilled of a hunter you are, if it is not there, you can't kill it. If there are very few elk in your area, it is going to be much harder to find them. Elk populations are not distributed equally among states, counties, mountain ranges, drainages, or hunting seasons, and they are very nomadic animals. There are vast amounts of hunting land, fragmented elk densities, and varying levels of antler quality disbursed unevenly among the patchwork of states and herds. Most of the areas elk inhabit are not considered quality hunting areas. Not to breed mistrust, but I would not plan a western hunt on any hunting area recommendation that is not supported by harvest statistics or personal experience. Personal experience means what you have physically seen first hand. You should not assume that elk will be in an area or obtainable through second hand stories. Too often hunters have no idea what the elk populations, densities, migration patterns, and hunting pressure is in an area before they trek across the country for a hunt. You can easily research and gather this information. The more information you gather, the better your hunt and more realistic your expectations will be.

Big Game Harvest Reports, Colorado Parks and Wildlife Website

So how does a hunter know where the good hunting areas are and how does a hunter know what areas should be avoided? To assist the hunting public, most states provide statistics directly stating hunter success rates, the amount of hunters, recommended areas, and the weather conditions of all hunting units within a state. This information is free of charge and posted on each state's respective State Wildlife Agency website. Navigating the websites is simple and you can always call the State Wildlife Agency directly to ask for directions in locating the information. Trust in these statistics and do not brush them off. Many hunters will be shocked to find how dreary the statistics are for the area they plan to go. The reality of it all is you will likely succumb to these statistics. Not accepting the reality of these facts will only lead to unrealistic expectations. If there is only a 10% success rate for where you plan to go, maybe you should rethink the amount of time and money you are devoting to this hunt. Or at the least do not let yourself become broken spirited without a harvest. Only one out of ten people harvest in an area with 10% success, one out of ten, how big is your hunting party? That number also includes the experienced locals and private ranches. The more you research, the better prepared you will be. The best course of action is to use these same resources to locate a much more desirable hunting area. The Research Scouting section of this book will thoroughly cover this concept and give specific recommendations on how to use hunter statistics.

Many hunters learn the previous lesson the hard way every year. When I first moved to Colorado I was very eager to begin hunting. I landed a job in a popular ski town that was surrounded by National Forest in all directions. I started scouting and hunting simply based on what National Forest access points were closest to my apartment. Without doing any research, I quickly bought the tags that were the easiest to obtain and that had the longest seasons. Why not? I thought elk were like whitetails and inhabited every stretch of forest around. As I began hunting, I was seeing more hunters than deer or elk and soon wondered how Colorado had developed a reputation for good hunting. I read the popular western hunting books, which primarily focus on hunting tactics, and I paid no attention to one of the most important themes in hunting: going to the right hunting areas. Finding the right hunting areas requires simple research. I didn't know that such information existed or that I should even be looking for it. My expectations were high, and the quality of my hunting experience was low. I didn't bag any game in my first year of western hunting. Seven tags, from elk to antelope, down the drain. I came to an obvious conclusion; whatever I was doing was wrong. I needed a western hunting education.

In the years since my early blunders, I have found continued hunting success and have guided many friends and family members to success as well. Nevertheless, as I begin discussing potential guided hunts with friends and family, the first thing I do is discuss statistics and expectations. Expectations are the starting point. If the realities of a potential hunt cannot reach a hunter's expectations, then either the hunt must be postponed until a better tag can be obtained or the expectations must be lowered. The only other choice is to not live up to your expectations, ensuring an unpleasant outcome.

The main idea behind managing your personal expectations is to educate yourself on your available hunting options. This may also mean educating yourself on a hunt you have already committed to next season. You need to have down to earth expectations for success grounded by the factual potential of your hunting area. If you spend time in preparation, information collection, and drawing the right tag, you can go on a hunt with soaring success rates, trophy class animals, and very high and accurate expectations in harvesting. It just takes time, planning, and patience.

Chapter 5 - Hiring a Guide

Before we get too deep into this reading, we should discuss the alternate approach to DIY hunting. That of course is to hire an outfitter or guide. There are both benefits and drawbacks to this course of action. First lets cover the drawbacks. In hiring a guide you forego the satisfaction of completing a successful hunt from the result of your own actions. Independently planning, implementing, and succeeding in taking an elk is a huge accomplishment. It fine-tunes your skills as a hunter and that of a problem solver. Lets face it, it does not require near the level of skill to kill an animal when you are fully guided. The burden and legwork rests on the shoulders of someone else. Similarly, the accomplishment can be mostly attributed to someone else. Guides and outfitters typically take care of just about everything for the client. When fully guided your duty is to follow directions and make a clean shot. While this is still not to be taken lightly, it isn't nearly the achievement of doing it independently and self-guided. Another drawback is of course the costs associated with hiring a guide. While costs between different outfitters do vary, you can count on a western fully guided hunt being pretty expensive. If you are curious about these costs, simply search for a few guides online to see what the price range is in a desired state.

If hiring a guide appeals to you, by all means do so. It is the simplest way for a novice to succeed. By doing so you are purchasing the expertise of a seasoned guide to complete all of the planning and resource gathering for you. In some situations it is very appropriate. If you feel overwhelmed, are out of shape, inexperienced, or elderly, it may be the safer option. Also, if hunting itself is a foreign concept to you and you don't have a mentor, it may be a better idea to have some direction on your first hunt. Maybe you don't have the time or resources to devote to planning your hunt and/or the hunt seems a bit too specialized. For international hunting, it is always a good idea. If for any reason you feel it entirely necessary, please do not let this book discourage you from hiring an outfitter. Guides and outfitters are seasoned professionals and repeatedly do what most of us struggle to do each year. Lets face it; this is a profession any seasoned hunter envies.

Another option is using an outfitter for a partially guided trip, such as a drop camp. Partially guided trips offer less guide services for less price. This mixes the benefits and drawbacks of hiring an outfitter. If such an arrangement interests you, many outfitters offer both fully guided and partially guided services. You simply need to inquire as to the services and details of partially guided trips.

Each year the majority of western hunters do not hire outfitters. Most of us simply cannot afford to hire an outfitter. With time and research success is very possible on our own and the rewards are much more recognizable. Nevertheless, guides are always a useful option and should be considered so while reading the rest of this book.

Chapter 6 - The License Game

Throughout this reading you will notice repetition of a few central themes. The next of which is drawing a quality tag. The repetition is intentional, as the importance of this theme needs to be emphasized. The tag you obtain is the most significant factor in your hunt. Your tag dictates where you hunt, when you hunt, and how you hunt. All hunting strategies, tactics, plans, and expectations are dependent on the tag you obtain. This is where you begin tag planning.

As mentioned, the success of your hunt is a direct result of the quality of your hunting area. Regardless of your hunting skills, your hunting will be much better if you are in a better hunting area. The tag you obtain will designate one or possibly a few game management units that you may hunt in. So how does one obtain a tag in a quality area? More often than not, the answer is through a tag drawing process.

Welcome to the **Arizona Game and Fish Department's Hunt Draw Application system**. The application period for the 2014 Pronghorn Antelope and Elk Hunt Draw is now available. If you would like more information on the draw, please visit http://www.azgfd.gov/draw

The hunt permit application deadline for the 2014 Pronghorn Antelope and Elk will be **Tuesday, February 11, 2014 by 7 p.m. (MST)**.

The last day to update your payment information will be **Sunday March 9, 2014 by 11:59 p.m. (MST)**.

Arizona Big Game Draw, Arizona Game and Fish Department Website

Most western hunters are overly familiar with the concept of tag drawing. However the purpose of this reading is to educate the beginner to western hunting, so this explanation will start from ground zero. For many entering the realm of western hunting the concept of limited entry tags is not fully embraced. In fact, first time western hunters often avoid it entirely. Perhaps this is due to the easy access of whitetail deer tags elsewhere in the country. Many hunters have never experienced having to apply through a lottery just to go hunting. The concept seems overly restrictive and very inconvenient. To be perfectly honest, it is. Even after you get used to doing it, it is still a pain in the ass. But the system exists for good reasons. There is a lot of demand for great western hunting units. If everyone who wanted to could hunt the best units, these areas would become over hunted. The fewer the hunters: the better quality of hunting in a unit. To provide perspective, this is why private land hunting is often better than public land hunting. Restricted hunter access allows for better management of game populations. Given the need for this limitation, the only fair method of providing public access is through a lottery or preference point system. In practical terms, this means a hunter needs to apply for tags well before seasons begin and accept the fact that coveted tags are not always attainable on an annual basis. Enter the license game. I call it a game because if you fall prey to the lure of western hunting you may find yourself comparing draw odds and unit data into the early hours of the morning. After applying, you may then find yourself anxiously awaiting draw results and celebrating with friends if successful in obtaining a tag. Simply put, there are more aspiring hunters than large bulls and bucks. With the majority of theses bucks and bulls living on public land, the only way to produce high quality public land hunting is to limit the amount of tags issued. In response, western states embrace a tag drawing process.

Let's look at a few of the benefits of limited entry tags. As mentioned, limited tag drawings decrease the amount of hunter pressure in an area. As a result of less pressure, elk have some beneficial behavioral characteristics. This means they operate in a much more natural state. With less hunter pressure, elk are more predictable because they are spooked less. They respond better to calling. They are more active during daylight hours. They are typically much closer to the parking access areas. Feeding and bedding areas are utilized by elk based on their habitat value rather than by their proximity to hunter access. Hunters in these units typically realize the quality potential and pass on the smaller animals. This results in older age classes of bulls. And the best part is that you avoid the intense competition from too many hunters. In highly pressured areas, I often find myself patterning and avoiding other hunters more than patterning the elk. With limited tags you may still have other hunters around, but the severity of this issue is greatly reduced. The bottom line is that you will see more game, encounter less competition, and increase your odds of harvesting a quality animal by obtaining a limited tag.

Before we go any further we should recognize that hunters do have the option to purchase over the counter (OTC) or leftover draw tags. By the time you are through with this reading I hopefully will have driven the point home that this is usually not the best idea. OTC tags pale in comparison to limited draw tags. Many hunters are attracted to OTC tags each year simply due to the ease of obtaining them. By doing so you avoid all the hassle and confusion of the license game and simply purchase a tag at a local outdoor store. Convenient-yes, but by doing so you have just forgone all the benefits of a limited entry tag. Countless hunters choose these tags solely for the convenience factor. Just because there is a lot of public land out West doesn't mean that it cannot become overcrowded. There are exceptions though. Some OTC tags can provide decent hunting. For instance, many OTC cow hunts are productive, as well as OTC hunts on private land. Sometimes OTC archery hunts can be quality, simply due to their being less people who archery hunt. But in general, OTC hunts are not correlated with quality game. If you buy a public land OTC tag, don't hold high expectations for a nice bull. OTC hunts hold the least amount of success and the most amount of hunter overcrowding. Do yourself a favor: avoid the crowds and put forth a little extra effort by putting in for the draws. OTC tags simply do not compare with the quality of limited entry draw tags.

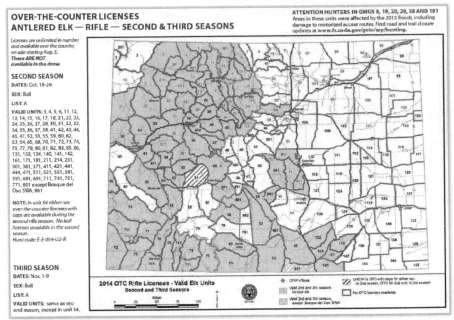

OVER-THE-COUNTER LICENSES
ANTLERED ELK — RIFLE — SECOND & THIRD SEASONS

ATTENTION HUNTERS IN GMUS 8, 19, 20, 29, 38 AND 191
Areas in these units were affected by the 2013 floods, including damage to motorized access routes. Find road and trail closure updates at www.fs.usda.gov/goto/arp/hunting.

Licenses are unlimited in number and available over the counter, on sale starting Aug. 5.
These ARE NOT available in the draw.

SECOND SEASON
DATES: Oct. 18-26
SEX: Bull
LIST: A
VALID UNITS: 3, 4, 5, 6, 11, 12, 13, 14, 15, 16, 17, 18, 21, 22, 23, 24, 25, 26, 27, 28, 30, 31, 32, 33, 34, 35, 36, 37, 38, 41, 42, 43, 44, 45, 47, 52, 53, 55, 59, 60, 62, 63, 54, 65, 68, 70, 71, 72, 73, 74, 75, 77, 78, 80, 81, 82, 83, 85, 86, 131, 133, 134, 140, 141, 142, 161, 171, 181, 211, 214, 231, 301, 361, 371, 411, 421, 441, 444, 471, 511, 521, 551, 581, 591, 681, 691, 711, 741, 751, 771, 851 except Bosque del Oso SWA, 861

NOTE: In unit 54 either sex over-the-counter licenses with caps are available during the second rifle season. No bull licenses available in the second season.
Hunt code: E-E-054-U2-R

THIRD SEASON
DATES: Nov. 1-9
SEX: Bull
LIST: A
VALID UNITS: same as second season, except in unit 54.

2014 OTC Rifle Licenses - Valid Elk Units
Second and Third Seasons

★ CPW offices
Valid 2nd and 3rd season; for bull elk.
Valid 2nd and 3rd season; except Bosque del Oso SWA
Unit 54 is OTC with caps for either sex in 2nd season, OTC for bull only in 3rd season
No OTC licenses available

Over the Counter License Map, Colorado

Thus far I have generalized tags as either limited or OTC. Not all tags in either of these generalizations are created equal. Limited tags range in price, quality, and draw odds. The governance of wildlife species falls to the jurisdiction of each respective state. Unfortunately, there is little uniformity in the application process from one state to another. Each state has its own set of rules and procedures in distributing game tags. However, there are a few similar concepts that the states embrace. It is the specific details on the implementation of these concepts that differs. As we begin to dig into common tag allocation process and hunting regulation generalizations, please keep in mind that regulations for each state change from year to year and the only definitive regulations are those formally published by each respective state on an annual basis. All applicable state processes regarding tags, units, applications, deadlines, and costs can be obtained through each states annual hunting regulation booklet or online from each state wildlife website. More and more states are relying on their websites to distribute information, but most will still mail the regulation booklet if requested. Just give them a call or send them an email.

Lets discuss the common tag allocation processes. Each state utilizes a different method for issuing tags. It can be very frustrating trying to keep up with the varied processes and continuously changing rules. Western states usually separate tags by species, weapon, and season. For perspective, many eastern states offer a single purchase deer hunting license that covers deer hunting throughout their seasons with multiple weapons. Such licenses may allow for multiple animals, i.e. a buck and a doe. As western states have multiple big game species and a high demand for hunting, specific animal tags are often issued instead of general licenses. The terms tag and license are sometimes synonymous and sometimes not. It simply depends on the subject state. If you are in Colorado, you must obtain a tag or license (synonymous here) for each specific big game animal you wish to hunt. In other states, tags might be required in addition to a hunting license. For example, in New Mexico a hunter must first purchase a general hunting license and then obtain a tag for each specific animal they wish to hunt, such as a bull elk or buck mule deer. For discussion purposes, I will just stick with the term "tag" when referring to both.

Tags are usually sex specific and singular. This means they are usually for one bull only or one cow only. In some cases, states will issue either sex tags, but these are still only good for one animal. In addition to being sex specific, tags are usually weapon specific. If you wish to archery hunt, you will need an archery tag. If you wish to rifle hunt, you will need a rifle tag. To complicate matters more, many states offer multiple seasons for each weapon type. In Colorado, there are four elk rifle seasons. Your tag allows you to hunt one of these seasons. So your tag is sex, weapon, and season specific. For example, you may obtain a tag that is a first rifle season bull elk tag. This tag allows you to harvest only one bull elk, in only the first rifle season. Some states allow hunters to use lesser weapons during the gun seasons. This means you can use a bow or muzzleloader during rifle season if you so choose, but you will need to make sure this is allowable in your state before assuming so.

The number or quantity of tags you may obtain is also limited. For instance, most states restrict a hunter to one bull elk tag in a given year. That means you cannot draw both an archery bull tag and a rifle bull tag in the same state during the same year. This is regardless of the number of tags to be issued in those units or whether or not you were successful in an earlier season. That means hunters must make definitive choices in tag applications as you usually can only draw one tag to hunt bull elk in each state. A few exceptions do exist where states offer tags in units that can be hunted with multiple weapon types and in multiple seasons. For example, Wyoming and Montana currently allow hunters to archery hunt with a general elk tag if they purchase an archery permit in addition to their general rifle tag. Hunters can then bow hunt in archery season and later rifle hunt during the rifle season if they failed to harvest with their bow. But this is not the norm, so be sure to check your tag restrictions specifically. While the tag quantity restriction is limiting, many states do allow hunters to obtain both a bull and a cow tag. You also have many species to apply for, as one species usually has no bearing on the others. For example, each year in Colorado a hunter may obtain what is called an "A" type tag and a "B" type tag for each different game species. "A" tags are usually for a bull or for either sex, while "B" tags are usually cow tags. In addition, you can try your hand at drawing deer, elk, pronghorn, moose, sheep, goat, and bear, as each species has no bearing on the other. Many avid Colorado hunters obtain two elk, two deer, two antelope, and a bear tag in Colorado each year. Sheep, goat, and moose are difficult tags to draw. This process applies in some form or another to the other western states as well.

Mule Deer, Colorado

So now that we know a little about what tags a hunter can obtain, let's talk about how many tags are issued. States take a biological and goal oriented approach to managing their wildlife. There are many influencing factors. These factors are too numerous to list, but I will attempt to generalize the main concept. Each state government has an agency dedicated to managing wildlife, and yes, each state has a different name for their agency. Some examples are Colorado Parks and Wildlife, Wyoming Game and Fish, Montana Fish, Wildlife, and Parks, Arizona Game and Fish, etc. Generally these organizations have a similar objective of managing wildlife and land in their respective state. For simplicity, lets just refer to them as the State Wildlife Agency. A significant number of State Wildlife Agency employees have ecology, biology, and natural science backgrounds. These employees utilize strategic methods to monitor, quantify, study, and manage the wildlife for its' health and longevity. Some examples of monitoring techniques are aerial herd counting, collaring and tracking game with GPS monitors, and hunter harvest surveys. These methods produce great statistical information regarding population health, size, behavior, and utilized habitat. The State Wildlife Agency then considers and often engages all interested stakeholders in wildlife management decisions. These stakeholders include hunters, farmers, landowners, the State Wildlife Agency itself, and even the general public. The State Wildlife Agency then considers the quantitative herd information, stakeholder interests, and current socioeconomic factors when making wildlife management decisions. The decisions of most interest to the hunting public are those of game population objectives, tag issuance, and hunting season regulations.

In a broad oversimplification, states usually take a stance of managing their game for what the hunting community refers to as either "opportunity" or "quality." When a state or unit within a state is managed for opportunity that means it issues a lot of tags, giving many people the opportunity to hunt. Opportunity units are known for having large elk herds but not a lot of mature animals. On the flip side, quality units value trophy potential over hunter opportunity. This means the number of tags is limited and the age class of animals is usually higher. As you can guess, the units managed for quality produce great hunting and are highly sought after. While this explanation is black and white, many states are somewhere in the middle. States often have a few units managed for quality, a few for opportunity, and a few in between. This gives a hunter a choice when choosing which tag to seek. Quality area tags are harder to draw while opportunity area tags are harder to harvest in. The ones in the middle are semi-difficult to draw and have moderate harvest rates. These middle grounds are a sweet spot for many western hunters as they can draw every few years and have decent hunting.

Whether units are managed for opportunity or quality, all states employ a system for tag allocation. A few states issue tags 100% randomly, others offer point systems, and some employ a combination of these two methods. The totally random draw system is the simplest. Everyone who applies has equal chance on a year-by-year basis. Odds of drawing are a direct result of the amount of people who apply and your odds are just as good as the next guy applying. The main advantage of this method is that you don't have to wait to build preference points and have a chance of drawing every year.

Point systems are much more complicated. The basic idea behind a point system is preference based on point accumulation. The more points you have, the better your odds in drawing. In general, an applicant may only obtain one point per year, per species, per state. They may do so by deliberately purchasing a point or by applying for a tag and receiving a point if they fail to draw. As you accumulate more points you become more likely to draw the tag. In some cases, individuals with the most points will be guaranteed a tag. For instance, if it is known as five point area, you will need to accumulate five points over five years and then you will be guaranteed to draw in the sixth year. These points are commonly referred to as *preference* points. This has obvious benefits in terms of planning. And yes, I did just imply that there are different types of points. In other cases, varying by state, having a point may place your name in the lottery one time for each point you possess. This increases your draw chance each year but does not guarantee a tag. These are commonly known as *bonus* points. This method is beneficial because you always have a chance at drawing and your odds substantially increase with the amount of bonus points you possess. However no point holder is guaranteed a tag and inevitably some tags will be issued to applicants with barely any points. In either case, when you draw, your points are purged. It doesn't matter if your tag required only one point and you actually had ten points. If you draw, all of your points are zeroed out.

Many states also allow for hunters to list a few tag choices on their applications. By doing so, a hunter can try for a first choice hunt and if they fail to draw they have a chance at possible second, third, or fourth choice tag. In this manner you are not betting on only one horse. Many hunters will put their dream hunt as the first choice and an acceptable hunt as their second choice. Some states consider all first choice applicants

47

before moving to second choice. Other states will open an application and if the first choice hunt quota is filled, then they will consider your second choice before moving to the next application. In the latter case, your second choice becomes more meaningful. Applicant beware, if applying for a second choice on an application, research whether a second choice success will purge your points. In some states it will, meaning if you wish to keep your points, don't apply for a second choice. In other states, only your first choice matters in terms of point retention. In this case, not drawing your first choice will gain you a point, and you may still draw and hunt your second choice tag. This is just another example of the differences between each state's processes, and more reason to read the regulations before submitting an application.

States also may employ a combination of the above methods. For instance, a unit may issue 80% of its tags to applicants with the most points and issue 20% on a purely random basis. Great units may require 15 to 20 points to guarantee a tag. Other units within the same state may be OTC, while others are draw but only require a minimal amount of points. Many tags can be drawn nearly every year, but are not sold OTC. A few states square bonus points to give higher odds to those with more points. In such cases, if you have 3 points accumulated, they would actually be worth 9 in the drawing.

Each state explains their system's details within their regulations and provides a breakdown of their units. They also denote drawing odds and required points for certain areas. While explanations are provided, the picture isn't always abundantly clear. Hunters jokingly admit that you need a PHD in tag regulations to fully understand the methods employed by each state. Specific point requirements are often generalized in the regulations, and a hunter must read between the lines for exact odds and point requirements. For this reason, many successful businesses have been started that specialize in simplifying state application and hunting data. In any case, read through the regulations of your prospective state to get the general idea, and feel free to inquire with the state agencies. Often times they have employees just for answering application questions. The resource section of this reading will go into the additional information sources you have to supplement the regulations. These resources will go into better detail as to specific unit odds and point requirements. With all processes and allocation methods considered, some states will be more appealing to you than others.

Limited entry units set a specified quota of tags to be issued each year. Now for some bad news, residents and non-residents are not treated equally. This is true in terms of price and tag quantity allocation. Non-resident hunting license prices can be astronomical compared to resident licenses. Often they are at least ten times more expensive. For example, in 2013 the price of a Colorado resident bull elk tag was $46. The same tag for a non-resident was $586. States also only allocate a small quota of tags for non-residents. Once this quota is reached, no more non-resident tags will be issued. Most non-resident quotas range in the 10-35% range. For example, lets assume a state allows for 15% of non-resident tags in a limited entry unit. If the unit issues 80 bull tags, a maximum of 12 licenses will go to non-residents. As soon as the 15% quota is reached, it doesn't matter how many points a non-resident has, no more non-resident tags will be issued.

Many states also offer landowner tags. This means landowners can apply for and receive guaranteed tags if they own a certain amount of acreage in a unit. The benefit of this is that many states allow these landowners to sell the tags on the commercial market. Purchasing one of these tags from a landowner usually allows a hunter to hunt anywhere in that specific unit without having to endure the draw process or lose any points. Drawbacks include purchasing the tag at a market rate and the fact that these tags lower the amount of tags to be issued in the competitive draw. Considering the non-resident drawbacks, there is one easy method to avoid non-resident prices and quotas. You simply have to move out West.

After looking through a couple state regulation booklets, you will be very surprised at the many tag options you have. There are easy to draw tags, once in a lifetime draw tags, and many in the middle. The choice is usually a matter of timing. If you want to hunt every year and cannot wait for a hard to draw tag, rest assured, this doesn't mean you have to settle for an OTC tag. There are many limited license drawings that have great chances of drawing every year, some even at 100%. Logic would tell you that these would be no better than OTC hunts, but interestingly enough these hunts still significantly have less hunters! People are much less inclined to send off an application in the months beforehand and would rather purchase their license the day before they take the field. If you want to hunt every year or if you must hunt a specific year, look for tags with a high drawing success rate that require minimal points. You will be much better off than an OTC tag. Or why not apply for that coveted draw tag and keep the OTC as your back up plan? If license quotas are not reached via drawing in an area, leftover licenses are usually issued and sold over the counter. As you can imagine, highly coveted tags never have leftover licenses. Leftover licenses are usually for cows, low demand areas, or in areas that need population reductions. Population reduction tags tend to be mostly cow tags as well.

Not every hunter is looking for the same type of hunt. Hunters need to decide what type of hunt they are looking for, consider all influencing factors, remain realistic, and then decide on what the right tag is for them. Please note that I stated you should be seeking the "right tag." This is a personal decision, as the right tag isn't necessarily the hardest tag to draw. Choosing the right tag is a combination of many weighted factors. Factors you will need to consider include weapon type, location, preferred weather, timing, terrain, and draw odds. All of these factors are influenced by many elements, and we will look at each in depth throughout this reading. Obtaining the right tag will also match your expectations with your success rate and provide a much more quality experience. Mismatching expectations and reality is mostly due to a lack of planning and experience, and often not even participating in the license game. Lets further this discussion by trying to determine what the right tag is for you.

States across the West offer a plethora of elk hunting options, some for opportunity and others for quality. Just about every state has a little of each. Ask yourself; do you want to hunt for opportunity or quality?

If you want quality, the path forward is quite simple. Minor research will reveal the best units and hardest to draw tags in each state. These tags will offer the biggest bulls, highest success rates, and least amount of hunters. The tradeoff is that obtaining one of these tags is difficult. In states where the draw is totally random, count on the draw odds being low, very low. In states that utilize a point system, you will likely have to build quite a few points to draw one of these tags. You will need to research how many points it takes to draw the tag you desire or the odds of doing so if it is a random draw. This will give you an idea of the waiting period you must endure before you go hunting in this unit. The earlier you begin this process, the better off you will be.

If you want to hunt strictly for opportunity, or immediately, you have many options. As mentioned earlier, there are many tags offered in many states with great drawing odds. Colorado, Wyoming, and Montana are notable for the amount of tags they issue through drawing to non-residents. Many of these tags require zero to one point. Such tags typically have large herds on vast amounts of public land. But don't expect it to be an easy hunt simply because elk herds are large in these areas. The ease of obtaining a tag also indicates that there will be many hunters in the woods. Albeit a good many less hunters than what you will encounter with an OTC tag. Research, scouting, and experience are your greatest allies with these hunts. Hunters will over concentrate in some areas. If you do your homework and avoid the crowds you will increase your success at harvesting.

Then there are the middle grounds. These are opportunities that capture a bit of both worlds. Just about every state offers units and associated tags that are moderately difficult to obtain. To illustrate, units may require 3-6 points or have random 5-30% draw odds. There will be many less hunters and many more bulls, but it still won't be a trip to the grocery store. These hunts typically have good bulls around, but not around every corner. It is a compromise of the quality and opportunity extremes, which is appealing to many avid hunters. You don't have to wait a lifetime and you still have a chance at a wall hanger bull. Nevertheless, you still have to play the license game to some degree.

The above three options are generalizations. But if forced to categorize the available tags in the West, this is a good method. As a prospective hunter, you need to decide what choice is best for you. Weigh the pros and cons of each option. Can you wait a lifetime for that amazing tag? Keep in mind that many of the best tags in the West can take 15-20 years to build the needed points. Can you wait 3-6 years for a quality tag? Or do you have the urge to get out in woods this year? If you must go sooner rather than later, you should consider looking into a tag that only takes a point or two to obtain. If you must go this year, explore a high odds draw tag rather than purchasing one over the counter. You will be surprised how much higher draw tag success rates are than OTC tags. You will also notice that I did not even recommend OTC tags in the above three options.

Now lets complicate things a bit more. In general, you have to set your sights on one tag for a given species in your target state. Ah, but there are many states that offer tags! Why not apply for that easy tag in one state and build points in another? That way you can hunt this year, and five years from now go on that quality hunt elsewhere. Maybe even set aside a state where you'll build points for that dream hunt that requires 15 points. You can easily adopt a different strategy for each state. You also have the option of changing your mind each year in the application process. If you want to cash your points in because you can't wait any longer, go for it. What you do in one state has no bearing on another. You can quickly multiply your chances of drawing tags by applying in multiple states. You can also build points in multiple states so that quality tags start to become available as you rotate hunting in different states. Pretty soon, you may find yourself with quality tag options maturing almost every year. But fair warning, if you do this be prepared to drop some cash in the license game.

Like many other avid western game hunters, I set my sights on multiple species in multiple states. The tags I target have different point requirements and draw odds in each state. Using this method, I tier my hunting strategy and attempt to go on a quality hunt every year. With the vast amount of state draw methods and tag options out there, you can easily devise a plan that suits your needs. The overarching question is always going to be, what are the odds of drawing this tag or how long do I have to wait to build enough points? The overarching question your wife will ask is why are you wasting all this time and money?

Hunters beware; playing the license game can be a costly venture. It is also a very dull conversation for anyone who is not an avid hunter, as I have been reminded of this many times by my fiancé. Each state has different prices to apply for licenses or to build points. Some states are much more expensive than others. Don't let the license game break your bank or put you in the doghouse. Make sure you include the cost of applications and obtaining points in your decision making process.

More and more hunters are playing the license game every year. Call it a side effect of globalization. Better technology, information, and communication have spurred the interest and ability of hunters to take their hobbies nationwide and even international. In the grand scheme of things, this means an overall lowering of draw odds. However game populations fluctuate as well. Elk herds are growing throughout the country, and reintroduction efforts are bringing game to new areas year after year. If you want to partake in a quality western hunt, the best approach is to begin planning years in advance. Formulate a tag drawing plan and start to build points for the future. Play the license game. After all, you can't win if you don't play.

Chapter 7 - Creating a Plan

The best way to begin planning a western hunt is to develop a tag strategy. Before you begin, you need to identify your specific hunting preferences and goals. The obvious goals are to have an enjoyable experience and harvest an animal. But perhaps you want to do so with a bow during the rut, or maybe you have a preferred terrain type in mind. There are many aspects of the hunt you will need to consider. In essence, you are beginning an internal questioning process that will guide your decision to apply for a specific tag. Before looking at actual tag options, you need to get a sense of your desired what, where, when, and how. To do so, ask yourself the below questions.

Creating a Plan Questions

1. Do I want to hunt for quality or opportunity?
2. Am I willing to wait to draw a quality tag or do I want to hunt next season?
3. What are acceptable hunter success rates for me?
4. What are acceptable draw odds in obtaining a tag for me?
5. How much am I willing to spend on licenses and applications?
6. Do I want to hunt elk that are feeding, rutting, migrating, or wintering?
7. What type of weather do I want to hunt in?
8. What type of terrain do I want to hunt in?
9. What type of weapon do I want to use?
10. Do I have the skills, ability, gear, and resources to make this hunt enjoyable?
11. Do I have realistic expectations?

Your answers to these questions are your starting point in hunt planning. This is where you begin the planning process. You likely will not have an absolute answer or preference to every question, and that's fine. You may even need to research the options before you know the answer to your own question. Some questions and answers will be more significant to you than others. For instance, you may want a quality tag with good draw odds regardless of weapon type. Or possibly you value a hunt in a pleasant climate with moderate terrain. Nevertheless, considering these aspects of the hunt will point you in the right direction and start to give you a notion of what you want to do. Specifically, the answers will help you make application choices, as your preferences will dictate where, when, and how you plan to hunt.

After you have some general ideas to the above questions, its time to start researching. Researching tags and making hunt preference choices should not be exclusive processes. As you look through tag options, certain facts may change your preferences or cause you to make a compromise. For instance, you may realize that draw odds are often better for archery hunting and decide that rifle hunting is not as important to you as your ability to quickly obtain a tag. Or you may realize that your weather preferences dictate what state and time of year you wish to hunt.

All of the research you complete on tag options should intertwine with your personal hunting preferences. You will soon find that your most significant preferences are focusing your search. You will then begin to narrow the options you are considering. Soon enough, you will find a tag that suits your needs. To the dismay of our wives, you will likely even find a few tags that you desire. For many hunters entering this realm, they wish to go hunting as soon as possible. Realizing the license game necessitates point building or a lot of luck, they set both short and long-term goals.

Take the advice of many western hunters and develop a tag strategy and long-term plan. It may consider just one or two states, or maybe multiple options between many different western states. A lot of hunters today develop a plan that incorporates multiple states, animals, and both short and long-term goals. It will truly assist your planning efforts if you write down or track your plan in some form or another. If you have a one time only hunt in mind, this may not be necessary. If you plan to do some long range planning, a written method to organize your plan will be helpful. One of the more popular methods is to utilize a Microsoft Excel spreadsheet to list your objective states, units, species, and points possessed. Organizing your efforts in this manner will also eliminate the need to replicate tag and unit research that you have already performed.

Like many hunters, I play the license game for multiple species in multiple states. I research both opportunity type hunts for the short-term and quality type hunts for the long-term. I have a simple Excel spreadsheet that lists the following information in column format for the tags I desire. The Excel spreadsheet tracks:

Whether I sent an application or not
State
Animal species
Unit
Weapon type
Season dates
Current points
Points required or draw odds
Application due date
Applications results post date
Cost
Refund amount
Whether I drew or not

In this manner I can organize the where, when, and how for both short and long-term tag objectives. It helps me to avoid research repetition and also lets me know how much money I am spending. I do not actually list application codes in my spreadsheet as these change from year to year. You are much safer looking those up in the regulations just before you send in your applications. The application due date column is also essential to ensure you don't miss a deadline. I entered the majority of this information during initial tag research years ago. Each year I look over the hunts to be sure that it is still what I desire and to make sure the information is still accurate. Sometimes you may change hunts, but the main legwork only needs to be done once. I also update the App. Sent column each year to know what applications I have sent so far that year, like a check box on a to do list. I then update the Draw Success column after the draw results are posted so I can see all my yearly hunts in one location. Just below my spreadsheet I also record state hunting identification numbers or state wildlife website log in information so I have everything in one place. Now this is a bit of overkill to some folks, but if you plan to play the license game in multiple states, organizing your efforts and coming up with a written plan such as this one is a very wise decision. Otherwise, information inevitably will be lost. There is no one correct method to do so, but at a minimum I recommend you record the species, state, and unit you are targeting, as well as the amount of points you have accumulated. Now let's look into the available tools to research tag planning and strategy building.

Chapter 8 - Research Scouting

What on earth is research scouting? Call it a side effect of technology advances and improved information sourcing. Hunters can now use many tools to plan their hunt long before they arrive in the field. Furthermore, hunters can perform very specialized research that previously required on the ground experience. This type of research is not always simple or precise, but it offers hunters a competitive advantage that simply did not exist in decades past. As we dive into this chapter, we explore grounds that are seldom discussed in common hunting literature.

A successful hunt begins long before you step foot in the field. Hunters today are utilizing pre-hunt research more than ever. It's hard to fathom that successful hunting can be so research heavy. Our romanticized hunting ideals lead us to believe the majestic hunt only involves the tactical stealth and skill of a hunter. Unfortunately this is not the case. Perhaps it was long ago, when the wilderness was unspoiled and the secrets of the backcountry were unknown. But this is not the reality we live in today. The land has been mapped. The animals are being managed. What lies behind the mountains is known. It may seem gloomy that much of the mystery and romance of the wilderness has disappeared, but the knowledge gained is only to the advantage of the modern hunter. Biologists, hunters, and state agencies have completed the in depth research. Technology has made the research results available to modern hunters. Many hunters each year still do chance upon trophies and find success, but hunters that research, plan, and strategize are finding success much more than those that do not.

The tools and resources discussed here are mostly for information gathering purposes. They point you in the right direction and help you in making pre-hunt decisions. First you need to locate the right area to hunt. This means choosing the right tag. This will ensure there is ample game in your unit and significantly increase your chances of seeing game. After you have your tag and know what unit you will be hunting, then you need to decide what specific locations within that unit you will be hunting. Remember, units can be very large with varied terrain. After you decide on the unit and location of where you will be hunting in that unit, then you worry about the specific hunting techniques to embrace. This bears repeating. The recommendation is that you spend more time on finding your hunting area than you do on learning how to call, glass, and stalk. While these tactics are important, they won't do you much good if hunting in a poor area. Research scouting places your focus on hunt planning. After you have crossed this hurdle, then worry about your tactics.

Many of the tools and resources used in research scouting are available free of cost. As you may have guessed, most exist primarily online. Yes, tag planning favors the computer savvy hunter. It also requires minor data analysis and map reading skills. The last two statements are probably not very welcoming for some hunters. Rest assured, many businesses offer services that do the legwork for you. You simply need to decide whether you wish to pay for these services or complete the research on your own.

Enough introductions, lets jump right in. Below is a list of the main resources you should embrace. It is by no means all encompassing, but it provides a hunter the detailed information they need to make educated tag and hunting strategy decisions.

Research Scouting Resources
1. State Published Yearly Hunting Regulations
2. State Wildlife Websites and Statistics
3. Application Service Magazines and Organizations
4. Online Searches for Articles, Websites, and Forums
5. Maps
6. State Employees and Forest Service Employees
7. Experienced Hunters
8. Hunting Books and Videos
9. Scouting
10. Hunting

Research and resource gathering take place in two interrelated phases. This is the tag-planning phase and hunt-planning phase. All of the above resources will be utilized in both phases; however you are looking for slightly different information in each phase. Given that the tag-planning phase takes place before the hunt planning phase, the first few resources mainly support the tag-planning phase and the latter mainly support the hunt-planning phase.

The tag-planning phase is where you begin. In this phase, you are researching the answers to the "Choosing a Tag" questions we discussed in the previous chapter. As a refresher, I recommend you reference those questions as you read over the below resources. It may also be helpful to jot your answers down to those questions. After you have an idea of your hunting preferences, your objective is to research, strategize, and apply for tags. The successful conclusion of this phase takes place when you secure your desired tag. At that point, the hunt-planning phase begins. Lets look at each of these resources in detail, beginning with those that support the tag-planning phase.

1. State Published Hunting Regulations

The top resource in every state is the official hunting regulations booklet that is released on an annual basis. As previously noted, this resource is utilized mostly in the tag-planning phase. If you plan to hunt in or are even curious about a specific state, reading their regulations is paramount. Not only do they dictate all processes and regulations for the respective state, it is also the official method of distributing the laws governing hunting in that state. In terms of credibility, all hunting related information takes a back seat to the regulations. The purpose of the yearly regulations is to stand as an all-encompassing hunter resource guide. It lists all regulations, yearly changes, available tags, seasons, weapons, laws, costs, everything.

A hunter's main use of the regulations is to view the details of the tags you may apply for. It does not provide any subjective information, recommendations, or hunting area preferences. It will however describe the processes involved with the license game for that state. As previously mentioned, the application and fee process is very different from state to sate. Ensure that you are well aware of the tag details and application/draw process before committing. Read about the costs involved. Take special note of the application deadlines. Many state regulations list draw odds and/or points required for specific hunting units. But the information is not always clear. We will touch on a better resource for this information in the state wildlife website resource section. In the regulations, you often need to read between the lines and make inferences to gather useful planning information. For example, the specific season dates will have a strong bearing on the weather you will encounter during your hunt. In general, the earlier in the fall the season is, the warmer the weather will be. Some states are inherently warmer or colder based on latitude, but the season dates will help you zero in what type of weather you will encounter.

New Mexico Big Game Regulations

Another essential tool the regulations provide is the game management unit map for each species in the state. This basic map is a reference tool you will use again and again. The location of each unit dictates its geography and land use. It gives you basic location data that you will later use to research public vs. private land, roads and access, boundaries, city/town proximity, weather, and topography. We will get into much more detail on mapping with a few later discussed resources, but the unit map is essential when narrowing down what area you need to closely research. When first looking through the regulations, you shouldn't be making any hard decisions based on the specific details of this map; it should only give you some generalized notions based on unit location.

New Mexico Game Management Unit Map

If you already know what state you wish to begin researching, browse the state regulations from cover to cover. Focus on pertinent sections and use the table of contents to locate answers to your specific questions. Look over the unit map to gain location information. Throughout the whole planning process you will refer back to the regulations for all your process, regulation, unit, and application questions.

Although this is where all tag data begins, the information is not detailed enough to make highly educated decisions. It is the first research resource because it contains the official regulations and tag information. Because it is the one official state information source, it ranks number one in hunt planning research. However, if you truly plan to weigh all your hunting options and to make well-educated decision, you should not stop with the regulation booklet. It is simply a reference guide to begin your research with.

The regulation booklet is distributed liberally through license sale outlets across its resident state. Some states only offer the regulations to non-residents electronically; others will send it to you in print by request. To obtain it electronically, you will need to download it from the state wildlife website for that specific state. To obtain it in print, simply call or email the State Wildlife Agency and request it be mailed.

2. State Wildlife Websites and Statistics

The next resource to discuss is the state wildlife websites. In my opinion, this is the best source of hunt planning information. Again, this resource is used primarily in the tag-planning phase. Similar to the regulations they contain a good deal of official information, but they also go much further to provide a surplus of research tools. Publicly funded agencies design these websites. Often the majority of their funding actually comes from the sale of hunting and fishing licenses. Based on that model, it is in their best interest to attract hunters and promote the longevity of the sport. This is also where you can draw down the regulations if not obtainable in print, but the regulations are just the tip of the iceberg.

Assuming you are planning a western elk hunt, let's walk through the steps to gather hunt planning information from this resource. To locate a state wildlife website, simply search for it online with your favorite search engine by typing "Wyoming State Wildlife website," or whatever state you wish to look up. The website should be easily recognizable and likely the first option to show up from your search. You will quickly notice these websites cover much more than hunting, such as fishing, state parks, outdoor news, etc., but they all have a specific section dedicated to hunting. It should be fairly simple to navigate to the hunting section of the website from the main webpage. Look for a link in the menu bar or navigation pane for hunting and click on it. After accessing the hunting area, you should see links to all types of hunting information. Now it is time to tinker around and absorb all the information you can. There may be educational videos, general species information, specific hunting tips and tactics, and biological data. Most states have different forms of promotional and educational media that aid hunters in being successful. At first you should be simply clicking around to see what is offered. Look through items such as game species field guides, how-to articles, herd mapping systems, recommended hunting areas, and statistical herd data. While much of the promotional media can be informative and entertaining, the information you should focus on is the statistical data. Remember, highly skilled biologists and ecologists are employed by these organizations that constantly monitor herd health and species populations. These efforts continuously result in statistical analysis and hunter friendly information that will educate the hunter in what is there, when it is there, and how you can hunt it. Lets examine how to use these statistics.

Much of the statistics of interest to hunters are obtained through previous season hunter harvest surveys. For example, after the end of a hunting season a state will send out a simple survey asking hunters what tag they possessed, if they hunted, how many days they hunted, and if they were successful. The aggregated data is then posted in a lengthy harvest results report. To find the statistics, search within the hunting section of the state wildlife website for links with key words such as statistics, harvest surveys, and harvest reports. You can often locate this information by typing such keywords into the state wildlife website search function or even by searching for it directly with an Internet search engine. When you find where the statistical hunting or harvest data is located, there are usually separate reports for each species in the state. Choose your species of interest and download or open one of the reports. In front of you is a long list of harvest data. The data is broken down into small sections. Each small section usually pertains to one unit or tag application code. A tag application code is the specific code used to identify a specific hunting season, e.g. first rifle bull elk. As each state may have literally hundreds of units or tag codes, these reports tend to be lengthy. Examine the information contained in the first section for the first listed unit. You should quickly be able to identify what the unit is and what type of information is provided for the unit. This is a prime example of when the regulations may need to be referenced for identification of unit and/or application codes. Having the regulations in hand during this process will help you identify exact hunts the information pertains to. Commonly included harvest information is amount of hunters, overall success rates, bull/cow/calf success rates, license/weapon type, and hunter days in the field. Looking through the harvest report, you will quickly discover how useful it is to compare this information from one prospective unit to another.

Sifting through such a large amount of information can seem daunting. In order to do so in a timely and organized manner, it is easiest to prioritize your efforts based on one specific data point. Consider your earlier answers to the *Creating a Plan Questions*. What type of data specifically appeals to you? Some of these data points will have more influence on you than others, but for most of us, the most significant factor is the unit's hunter success rate. Lets focus on this data point for discussion purposes and disregard all others for the moment. A simple method to sift through the data is to quickly scroll through each page and take note of the units or codes that have high hunter success rates. For perspective, anything higher than 30% is pretty good for elk hunting.

Browsing the data, pick a success rate that is desirable to you and narrow your search to only units with that rate as a minimum. Note or highlight these unit numbers as you scroll through the report. Only highlight those that meet your minimum. You may have to increase or decrease your acceptable rate based on the amount of units that make the cut. Try to limit your highlighted units to a reasonable amount, such as five or ten. After you have these units highlighted, look at the accompanying data in the units you have identified. Now it is time to consider your hunt preferences. Perhaps they have the data broken down by season and weapon type. In such cases you should either gravitate to the weapon of your choice or to the season with the highest success rate, depending on your preference. The season with the highest success rate may imply when animals are in a given area based off of migration patterns, rut activity, or an earlier season when the animals have yet to be pressured. If they list the number of hunters, continue to narrow your search to the units with fewer hunters. If they list hunter days in the field for success, further narrow your search based off units with the least amount of days in the field. Look for the units that have the highest herd populations. The reports may list averages over time, or have a separate report for each year. Use logic to best strategize your unit preferences based on all of the data that is provided. Remember, not all state websites post the same information, and some reports are much more user friendly than others. You need to look over everything that is offered and take it for its value. Soak in as much as you can. Pick out the top few units or application codes that interest you. For exercise purposes, lets say you opened the statistics for Colorado and looked over the units for five year success rates over 30%. Upon doing so, you then noted the ten highest from that list. You then further narrowed down these highlighted units to only those with first season rifle hunts at this success rate. With these in mind, you picked out the top three success rate units. At this point, you would now have three preferred hunts in mind to explore further. You don't have to stick to three, but you should definitely have multiple choices in mind. This is the type of analysis the statistics allow you to complete. This method of choosing a hunt is much more fact based than simply taking a third hand recommendation.

With a few statistics based hunts in mind, let's take the information a bit further. In a similar fashion to harvest statistics, states usually issue tag drawing data in a posted report. Statistical herd and hunter information is usually posted separately from tag drawing data, but not always. Some states even post it in their regulations. Locate the report as you did for the harvest statistics. Open the report and look to the units that you highlighted from your previous research on success rates, hunter numbers, herd size, etc. The information in the drawing report or summary will once again be broken down by unit or application code. This data is somewhat simpler. It will detail the amount of tags issued, the amount of hunters who apply, and your chances of drawing a tag or the points it will require. The exact odds may be listed here, or you may need to complete a simple division problem to obtain the draw odds or points required (i.e., divide the number of tags issued by the number of first choice applicants). This type of information usually doesn't change too much from year to year, but be sure you check current year data just to make sure. Jot down this information next to the top three units or application codes you previously wrote down. Now you start to see a bigger picture. You now know the success rate and statistics of your desired hunts, and you also know your odds or waiting period in obtaining the tag. If your top three choices are difficult to obtain, you may want to rethink your top three choices. Often the best hunts take much longer to obtain than hunters want to wait. In such cases compromises must be made in the quality of the tag to be applied for. You can work your way down through your desired list, based on success rates, to find a tag that is obtainable in the time period you desire. Perhaps you would rather start with narrowing your search based on the time it takes to draw tags, then move to the statistical harvest data. Whatever you prefer, you should get an idea of how you can use the state wildlife website statistical data to search for tags that interest you. Your tag choices may shift in preference, but all the information you need to make educated decisions is provided for you. The playing field for the license game is set; it's just a question of how much effort you wish to put forward to find the best tag to apply for.

The former data analysis processes may seem overly complicated and difficult. You are right, it is not as simple as many of us would like. But you should find solace in the fact that most hunters are not doing this type of research. Actually looking at the data and making educated choices based on statistics will give you a competitive edge. To prove this point, look at a few of the units that have terrible success rates and high hunter densities. For many hunters that do no research, this is where they end up hunting, simply because they were oblivious to the statistics and what their options are. Putting a few hours of research into tag planning is much better than a weeklong hunt without seeing much game. Not to mention all the foregone costs associated with an unsuccessful elk hunt.

After you work your way through the regulations and state wildlife website statistics, you have actually done most of the research in tag preparation that you will need to. The data has been mined. You can access data on the best areas and what is involved in obtaining a tag for them. All other resources we will go over are gleamed from this information or simply supplement it. You can even replicate your efforts from one state to another for comparison purposes. Do your top three choices in one state look much better than your top three choices in another state? Maybe you will decide that one state is not worth applying in at all. Maybe you will decide that one state has a great long-term tag, and another has a great short-term tag. Like many license game addicts, maybe you will adopt a strategy that encompasses multiple states, species, and goals.

Looking through the state wildlife website statistical data is time consuming and sometimes overwhelming. In spite of this, these are objective statistics that remove personal bias. You are basing your general tag choices off of data, not hunches or tips. It is not the sole source for choosing tag, and yes, bad units may have good areas within a unit. However that is typically the exception. Statistical information will get you into the right units. This is the top resource in unassisted hunt research. While it is not perfect data, it is certainly the best that is offered. All of the statistical information is provided free of charge, and is at your fingertips with a few clicks of a mouse. It is a simple personal choice to use it or not. If the first hand data analysis process seems unwelcoming, the next resource may be your answer.

3. Western Application Magazines and Services

Once again, this is a resource used primarily in the tag-planning phase. There is cult following in the hunting world today. Well, maybe we are not a cult, but we certainly are obsessive. DIY western game hunting is addictive, and there is a very strong demand for it in the US. Coupled with the demand for western hunting is a demand to hunt in the best areas. This is certainly demonstrated by the terrible draw odds in the more coveted hunting areas. But sifting through harvest statistics, biological herd data, and ever changing state application regulations as described in the first two resources is complicated and time consuming. Recognizing this demand as a business opportunity, organizations have emerged that do all the tag and application legwork for consumers. These organizations offer two types of services: *tag recommendations* and *application submissions.*

If paging through multiple state regulations and sifting through harvest statistics is not your ideal way to spend free time, these services are your answer. First lets discuss organizations that offer *tag recommendations*. These services are usually offered by magazine or online. Using statistical information offered by state wildlife agencies and various other industry resources, these organizations analyze and publish hunting unit recommendations for just about every western state. In a nutshell, they take all the hunting regulations and statistics from each state and simplify, summarize, and organize them for readers. Rather than providing all the fine print and data for a whole state, they simply list what is the most relative to hunters. They then provide recommendations as to the best hunting areas for each state, species, and weapon type. Just about everything you need to know for application decisions in each state is contained in these magazines and websites. State by state comparisons, seasons, costs, recommended areas, and hunter testimonials are provided. Everything previously discussed that you will need to research on your own is provided with a subscription price. While the statistics are provided to the public by each state free of charge, you will quickly learn it is quite a task to organize all of them on your own. Application service organizations do all of this for you in a very appealing, user-friendly, and professional manner.

Eastmans' Hunting Journal, Issue 141

To take the processes one step further, many organizations will even submit hunting applications for you. This is known as an *application submission* service. If you do not wish to ever deal with the ever changing application codes, submission dates, and confusing regulations, these organizations will send all your desired applications in for you.

Moreover, the individuals submitting your application are seasoned experts in the best application choices given your goals and objectives. Essentially, these organizations ask you a series of questions similar to what you asked yourself in the *Creating a Plan* question list. They then consider all of your preferences and make educated application decisions. This removes all complexity and effort for the hunter. Many hunters employ these services every year.

If you truly wish to simplify the license game and would like the opinion of industry experts, these services are the way to go. They essentially do the research for you. Based on their recommendations, you can narrow your application choices down in a fraction of the time and also rest assured that all options were considered. Many subscribers utilize the tag recommendations service and send in their own applications. While their recommendations are extremely useful, you will still need to rely on the regulations and the send in your applications. Other hunters get the full package application service and remove themselves from the process completely.

Huntin' Fool Magazine, Volume 19 Issue 2

If you choose to use these services, then utilizing their recommendations becomes the first step in the tag planning process. This means you can skip over the first two covered resources and simply read tag recommendations given by the experts. It certainly does save a lot of time in terms of research and organization. Most who subscribe to these services swear by them. They are not only helpful, but very entertaining as well. A quick Internet search with your preferred search engine will populate many of these organizations. If you choose to go with one, read what a few competitive services have to offer to determine which one is right for you. Although many companies exist, *Eastmans' Hunting Journal* and *Huntin' Fool* magazine continue to be the industry leaders. You should consider their services, prices, and your own situation when choosing to subscribe. Bear in mind the objective statistical data is offered by the state wildlife agencies free of charge. These organizations are providing a service that organizes it, presents it in a comparative manner, offers their recommendations, and will even send in your applications if you wish. Check out what they have to offer, even seasoned DIY guys can use a hand every now and then.

4. Online Searches for Articles / Websites and Forums

Basic online searches are an interesting tool that can definitely be classified as optional. This tool is more useful in the tag planning phase, as it usually only provides general knowledge, but you can also employ it in the hunt planning phase. It is not as important as other resources, but it doesn't require much effort so it's always worth trying. Online searches can be hit or miss, as they are only helpful if past hunters or outdoor writers actually took the time to write and publish information online about hunting areas. The information is also second hand and subjective in nature. For that reason, you should take it all with a grain of salt. Nonetheless, it can provide general knowledge or indicators of hunting unit realities. The information also depends on the usefulness of search engine results and the ability to navigate multiple website articles for valuable information. It is placed fourth in the order of resources not out of significance but rather by when it is employed in the planning process.

In using this tool, the first thing you need to decide is what type of information you are looking for. Once again, open up your favorite online search engine. Search engines use the key words you entered and match them to online websites. The more generic your search, the more generic results you will receive. For instance, if you are considering what state to hunt in, you may try a search for "best elk hunting state." A search this generic is going to produce multiple online hunting articles, online forums, and even outfitters. But a search such as "hunting Arizona unit 10" will narrow your results to only articles pertaining to that unit. After you type in a search, open each article briefly to see if it contains useful information. You should be able to note rather quickly if the information is useful or not and simply move onto the next site if it isn't what you are looking for. Online articles published by noteworthy magazines and websites often contain practical information. Forums and blogs usually contain hunter posted information. This hunter information is highly opinionated but it should provide general notions, especially if the same opinions are consistently stated. If you already know what state you wish to hunt in, you can try to narrow your search by "best areas to hunt in Wyoming," or "best Wyoming general license hunting areas." If you know what unit you wish to hunt in, try searching for it, such as "hunting Wyoming unit 7." The more specific you are, the more specific results you will obtain. However, specific searches also have less information posted. I used Wyoming unit 7 as an example because it is a quality hunting area. Searching for notable hunting areas will produce more search results, as they are a constant conversation in the hunting community. You can also slightly modify your search language to seek different results. Try both generic and specific keywords, and tailor your search language based on the results you are receiving. The more you modify your search language and click around through different websites, the more should notice repetitive information. Repetitive information is what you should be looking for. For example, searching for the best elk hunting state will undoubtedly reveal a few top named states with consistency. Then combine this information with what you have already gleamed from your other tools to gain useful knowledge. For instance, online searches will surely state Arizona as having amazing hunting; your statistics research will tell you that it takes many years to draw a tag in Arizona's coveted areas.

We should take a moment to discuss online forums. This is a unique communication tool that you can read or participate in. Multiple websites host these forums. If you wish to utilize them you will need to choose the ones that you believe are the most noteworthy. At these websites hunters discuss their tactics and past experience in states, units, and on specific hunts. You can simply read over what has been posted or you can ask questions or give answers yourself. Hunters don't want to give away their secrets, but general information, such as if they were successful, when to go, and if they would recommend a unit, usually is not very hard to divulge. You can easily communicate back and forth with hunters on these forums. Keep in mind that this is sensitive information, so be respectful.

An online search for hunting information is a tool that is expanding as our use of the Internet grows. It is only as reliable as its' source, and that's often an anonymous blogger. Nonetheless, it can provide general notions or specific opinions that cannot be obtained through other means. It is most useful in the tag-planning phase, but you can also revisit this source in the hunt-planning phase. It is free of charge and very easy to access. The only issue is the quality of information. Use this information only to supplement your other data. Time spent with this resource should be limited, and it is certainly more of an optional source. Nevertheless, utilizing all the information available to you will only increase your knowledge base for a potential hunt, so why not give it a try.

5. Maps

After state wildlife statistics, maps are your next best planning resource. Maps are used heavily in both phases of the planning process. We will go into a good bit of detail with this resource as maps are used for many purposes. DIY western hunters are map-reading addicts; it's just the nature of the sport.

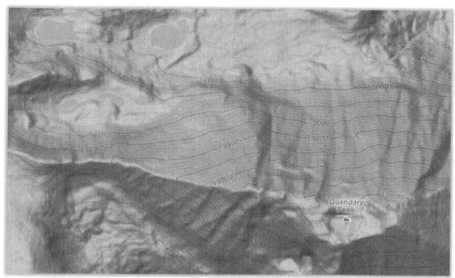

Contour Lines on Google Maps

The ability to read a topographical map is a very wise skill to have as a western hunter. These maps are not complicated. A quick glance at one will reveal many small parallel lines over the geographical features. These are called *contour lines* and their purpose is to show elevation and topography. The distance between each line represents the same amount of elevation gain when you move perpendicular from one line to the next. When placed further apart, the land has little rise. When close together, the terrain is steep. Elevations are stated on specific contour lines at set intervals. Use the stated elevation lines as reference and the ascending contour lines to see how varied the terrain is. Close circular lines form hills and mountains and spaced straight lines form flat terrain. Western hunting takes place on large tracts of land and using the contour lines on a map paints a three dimensional picture of the land you are looking over. This is a very brief explanation, but as you look over a topographical map you should quickly pick up on the concept. If not, there are many online or text resources to assist in map reading skills. You will use maps to help choose a unit, where to hunt within that unit, and to guide you while hunting. Lets discuss why we use maps as well as the types of maps to use.

In the tag-planning phase, maps are used very briefly and the information you need to gain is very basic. Because the information to be gathered is basic, online mapping is the easiest resource to utilize. Online mapping resources are free as well. Remember, in tag-planning you are simply choosing the right tag to apply for, you are not planning out a hunting strategy. That being so, many DIY hunters are looking for one thing in this phase: accessible public hunting land. The western states are covered with public lands, but not all are created equal. There are many different types of public land, but the majority of public land conducive to hunting falls into four categories: National Forest, BLM land, National Wildlife Refuges, and state land. For discussion purposes, we will just focus on these four categories. Of these four, the most targeted elk hunting land is National Forest. National Forest is usually mountainous-forested terrain, which is the type of habitat elk prefer. BLM land is often at slightly lower elevations than National Forest. Sometimes it's forested; sometimes it's not. In the West, lower elevations receive less precipitation, but don't count out BLM land simply because it is often more arid than National Forest. BLM land makes up great hunting land across the West. It just has a tendency to be at slightly lower elevations than National Forest. Compared to National Forests and BLM land, National Wildlife Refuges are few and far between. These have location specific hunting rules, but some National Wildlife Refuges are renowned for their great hunting. Individual refuges can be quite sizeable as well. It really just depends on the specific location and habitat. Lastly, we have state hunting land. State hunting land takes many shapes and forms. Some of it is owned directly by the state, while some of it may be leased by the state for public access. This type of land is generally in much smaller tracts. Its quality of habitat is going to be location specific. Often this type of land is used in conjunction with the other public land types, such as providing access to National Forest or for other outdoor recreation purposes (e.g., fishing, hiking, biking, etc.). Be sure to look into the specific rules and regulations of each state land site, as rules can even vary depending on the time of year. Your mapping efforts will need to seek out these types of public land for your hunting needs.

Most avid western hunters adopt personal map usage techniques to search for public land. This reading gives a rudimentary technique and should help you develop your own method. To begin, you will need to know what area you are looking into to check the availability of public land. By the time you reach the map resource stage, you should have a targeted tag in mind based on your earlier efforts. That tag will list the specific unit or units it allows you to hunt in. Access the state regulations via the regulations booklet or state wildlife website and open up the hunting unit map. This map was discussed briefly in the regulations resource section. Be mindful that some states have different unit maps for different species. Access the unit map you need and have it present for this process. Sometimes the unit map shows general public and private land boundaries, but often they are not very detailed. To ensure you have ample and accessible hunting access you will need to compare these unit boundaries to a better-detailed map. The first and easiest resource to use for this purpose is *Google Maps*. Google Maps does a great job of showing National Forest land and most National Wildlife Refuges. As National Forest is often the primary target of hunters, it is a good place to begin. The other land types will need to be accessed through different maps, which we will discuss in a moment. Search for Google maps with your favorite search engine and open it up. Google maps offer a "map" view and a "satellite" view. The viewing option can be changed by clicking either the "map" or "satellite" viewing option button in the top right corner of the window. The map view depicts land type; utilize this view rather than the satellite view. Quickly move the Google map to the state and location of the hunting units you have referenced on your unit map by dragging the map with your mouse and zooming in. You can zoom by double clicking on any specific location. You should be able to reference towns and roads in your targeted unit to get generalized locations between the two maps. Within a few moments you will notice that the National Forest areas in Google maps are highlighted in light green. The boundary lines of the National Forest in Google maps are only approximate, but you can count on them being accurate within a few miles. For tag planning, this level of accuracy is good enough. Looking closely, how much National Forest resides in your unit? Some units are almost completely National Forest, while others may have little to none at all. Ample National Forest for DIY hunting should be comprised of multiple mountains and drainages. After determining the amount of National Forest, zoom closer to ensure there is ample road access. Ample road access simply means there are multiple public roads entering the National Forest. Hopefully there is plenty of National Forest and plenty of roads accessing it. This means you will have multiple hunting location options in your unit. The less road access there is, the more hunters will pile up in the same areas. Repeat this process for National Wildlife Refuges as well.

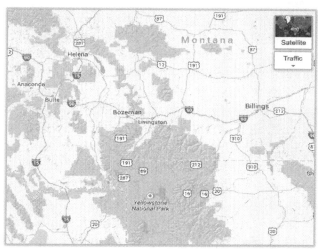

Public vs. Private Land on Google Maps

If National Forest is not located within your hunting unit, the battle is not lost. Overall, BLM land actually encompasses more public land than National Forest; it just isn't shown on Google maps like National Forest is. I only mention Google maps first because it does well to show National Forest and has great search and zoom functions. If you are looking for a map with all federal lands, a quick Internet search for a public land map will pull up everything you need for tag planning. Simply open up your favorite search engine and search for "Colorado public land map," or whatever state you wish to research. There are both government operated websites and private companies that offer easy to use online maps that outline all types of federal land. The general maps provided by *nationalatlas.gov* and *publiclands.org* provide all the mapping tools you will need for tag planning. Remember, a basic map depicting land type is all you need to determine if there is ample public land where you will be hunting. Once again, use your unit map as a location reference and check your specific area for public hunting land. On many maps National Forest is depicted in green and BLM is often depicted in yellow. Maps may show many different types of federal land so check your map legend for the specific land type identification. Hunting is generally allowed on all National

Forest and BLM land. Other types of land may have varied usage rules. If these maps are not very detailed, that's okay, you are simply checking to ensure there is ample public land and access to it in the target units from your desired tag. You are not planning specifically how you are going to hunt, but rather that you will have ample opportunity to hunt.

Finding state land maps can be a little more difficult. Accessible state land changes from year to year so many national websites do not cover them. To find the areas specifically open to hunting, your best resource for locating usable maps is the state wildlife website. Navigate to this website and look for any links referencing land usage or maps. This could be links for state parks, state wildlife areas, state trust lands, hunter access programs, etc. Remember, states receive a lot of revenue from the sales of hunting licenses; often they use this money to make more land available to hunters. If you are having trouble locating these maps, utilize the search engine on the state wildlife website or give the agency a call. Odds are that a mapping tool exists; it just may not be that easy to find on their website. Let's assume you located the map or maps that depict state lands. Once again, quickly look over this land to ensure there is ample hunting terrain and ample access to it. Use your unit map as a reference to find your target unit. Read the site-specific regulations for that tract of land to ensure it will work out for your hunting needs.

In addition to searching for land and access to it, at this point you may want to pay some attention to elevation and topography. Your investigation should not be arduous, as you are simply ensuring this is a doable hunt and therefore a tag you wish to apply for. Nevertheless, if you do not want to hunt at a high elevation or in too steep or difficult terrain now is the time to do a brief check. An easy method to do so is to fire up Google maps once again. If you were already using it to look over the National Forest then you should have your unit located already. Use the "terrain" feature to activate contour lines and elevation labels. Similar to the map and satellite views, the terrain feature is a viewing layer within the map view option in the top right hand corner of the website window. You may need to hover over the viewing option boxes for the feature to appear. Once activated, look generally over the public land where you wish to hunt. Is it high in elevation? Is it extremely steep? Ensure that you are comfortable hunting at the elevations where the road access enters the public land and for a few miles deep into it. The closer contour lines are to one another, the steeper the terrain. In general, steep terrain is physically demanding to hunt in. You can also use the "satellite" function to get an actual view of the land. If you were utilizing a different type of map to check for public land, check to see if it had contour lines and elevation labels. If so, briefly look over the land in the same manner described above. If it is not detailed enough, simply use your map, or the regulation unit map, to reference your location and open up Google maps to check the terrain and elevation. Elevation will also have a bearing on weather and temperature. You can locate the nearest town and research the average temperatures and precipitation for that time of year. *Wikipedia* and *weather.com* both offer this information by searching for the closest town on their respective websites. During tag planning, general notions should be guiding your choices and you don't need to split hairs on any of this information. Consider the amount of public land, access to it, difficulty of the terrain, and the weather. Ensure that the general information gleamed from the map can produce an enjoyable and doable hunt.

Thankfully, there are millions of acres of public hunting land in the West. While the procedures described above are not overly scientific, they give you a general process and you can hone your research from there. Online mapping resources are not always perfect, but you should be able to locate a unit and tag with ample public access. Often units have a conglomeration of many different land types that allow hunting. For instance, BLM land may back up to National Forest land and certain areas of it may be joined by state land. Sometimes hunters may utilize different land types during hunts for different reasons. For instance, I have stayed in camper cabins in state parks while hunting on nearby National

81

Forests. A hunter should investigate the opportunities of all land types before venturing out. There is probably more hunting land in a unit than you realize. Remember, locating a desired tag should begin with statistical investigation on hunter success, pressure, and tag availability. After you have a few tags in mind then you use maps to ensure there is ample access to public land and that this is a physically desirable hunt. These are general tag planning notions; the upcoming hunt-planning phase serves a completely different purpose.

We will briefly touch on a few instances when the next few resources can be used for tag planning, but for the most part this ends the tag-planning phase. The conclusion of the tag planning phase is signified when you actually apply for your tags either online or through the mail. Most states are embracing online application systems now. These tend to be easier to use than the traditional mail-in applications as they can identify errors before submission. Nevertheless, you will need to check the states regulations for the appropriate method in submitting your applications. In your regulation research should have also noted application submission deadlines as well as when the drawing results are posted. Make sure you are very aware of these dates. Precious points can only be accumulated at a rate of one per year. Losing one year can really hurt in the long run. Once applications are submitted, the waiting game begins. Best of luck!

So far all resources we have discussed have been for tag planning. As we move down through the list, now we begin to phase into hunt planning. After researching all the available information in the tag-planning phase, hopefully you found a few tags that interested you. Moreover, with any luck you obtained one. In any case, we are going to assume you have a tag in hand at this point. Many hunters do not spend much time on hunt planning until they actually draw a tag. This is for good reason, as the time may be wasted if they do not draw, and it can take years to draw some tags. Most states post the results of their draw in late spring to early summer. This gives the hunter a good bit of time to plan out their hunting strategy before the season opens.

Lets assume you just checked the draw results and were successful. So what do you do now? Well we are still within the mapping resource, so you can guess what the first recommended resource to utilize is. Previously we discussed using online maps for referencing available public land. Now that you know the unit or area you will be hunting, the end goal is to narrow it down to specific hunting locations. But lets not get ahead of ourselves. Hopefully your research led you to a tag in a unit with ample public hunting land and good access to it. With many hunting options, you want to ensure you are making a very educated decision on where to specifically hunt within your unit. Assuming you have never hunted this area, you should not be attempting to find only one location to hunt. Without boots on the ground experience in a unit, you should identify multiple location options that look appealing. After you have multiple locations in mind, you will eventually narrow them down further with additional resources or by actually scouting in person. But for now, the task is to scout with a map.

Before we get into scouting your location with a map, you are going to need a good map to scout with. Google maps is always a great tool, including Google Earth. Google earth goes one step further than Google maps in that you can get a better satellite view of terrain and view it from multiple angles. Other online topographical maps can be a great resource as well. Nevertheless, when actually scouting an area with a map, I prefer to use a good hard copy topographical map. I then use that map in conjunction with online mapping tools, such as Google maps and Google earth. Survey five western hunters on who makes the best hard copy hunting maps and you will get five different answers. There are a lot of options, and you will need to choose what map is best for you. Some good choices are those offered by BLM, the National Forest Service, and by National Geographic. Many other organizations offer maps tailored just for hunting, such as the popular *DIY Hunting Maps* or *Flatline Maps*. Look over a few maps to see which you prefer. A quick online search will turn up multiple options for you. Just be sure the map shows public land boundaries, access roads, and elevation topography. The map should also be at a usable scale. I prefer the scale to be at 1:50,000 or larger. A larger scale map will have less area depicted, but the detail will be much greater. For hunting purposes, it is better to own two maps at a large scale than one at a small scale. Maps showing vegetation are very helpful as well. As this map will likely be in your pack while hunting, those that are more durable and waterproof get extra points.

So how does one scout with a map? It's not as hard as you may think. You are simply narrowing down your choices for when you actually get to your unit. Depending on the hunter pressure and season you are hunting, you will need to look for certain features. There is a lot of land out there and western game has much smaller population densities than eastern whitetail deer. Therefore the game has their choice of land and you need to predict where they will be. You are going to be hunting large tracts of land and travelling long distances. Do not simply look for hot spots close to your parking area; areas further from the access points tend to have less pressure. You need to go to the elk; they are not going to come to you.

On a side note, many hunters decide they wish to car camp or park a trailer at the exact location of their hunt. While this is obviously convenient for many reasons, it can also be very limiting. Not all National Forest roads allow camping, trailers, fires, etc. Those that do allow camping often stack up with hunting camps. If you are camping or using a trailer as your base, don't limit yourself to only hunting from your camp as an entry point. You can easily camp in one location and drive to another to actually hunt.

Okay, back to using a map for scouting purposes. When looking through your map for hunting areas, the first item to consider is the time of year you are hunting and how the animals will be utilizing the terrain. Earlier in this reading we discussed how elk utilize different elevations during different seasons. You will use this knowledge and the time of year you are hunting to make educated guesses as to whether the elk will be utilizing high feeding elevations, rutting middle elevations, migratory areas, or low land wintering areas. Elk

84

move from high to low elevations depending on weather and pressure. If the elk do not migrate in the area you are hunting, you may not have to pay as much attention to the movement factor. Most western game does migrate to some degree, or at least change their habits depending on the season. Specific elevation usage is relative to a given area. Thus the terms, high, middle, and low elevation should be applied to a general region of your hunting state. For example, a high elevation is higher in Colorado than in Montana, but the animals use it in a relative manner. All elevation zones may exist within one unit, or maybe just one.

As a refresher, elk tend to prioritize feeding in the August to early September time frame (high elevations). They then move into various rutting stages for the duration of September and into early October (middle elevations). After the rut wanes the elk begin to concentrate on resting and feeding before the winter sets in, usually for the remainder of October (middle elevations). Migration timing is location specific and depends on the severity of weather (i.e. snow), and human pressure. Elk usually travel on traditional routes (migration corridors) and move to the low land wintering grounds (low elevations) by the time around 18 inches of snow falls. Snows at high elevations remain all winter long, thus elk usually do not stick around once deep snow builds up. Depending on specific location factors, the snows and migrations begin anywhere from late October to December. The distance of migration is also location specific. Human pressure is the curveball characteristic that will occur based on the hunting pressure in each area and hunting season. When pressured, elk simply move to areas where they are not pressured. This could mean areas that are far from roads, trails, and access. Often this means moving to their low elevation wintering grounds or simply to close by private land.

Based on the elk behavior and primary motivations during the time of year you are hunting, look at your map and try to get a sense of what areas the elk will be utilizing. You can make a judgment call as to the relative elevation based on what the elk behavior will be for that time period. If it is late August to early September before the rut, the elk will have established bedding and feeding patterns at high elevations. Feeding may occur above tree line, on open slopes, or in very high alpine valleys. The elk will likely bed apart from their feeding areas, but a couple miles distant at most. Bedding areas tend to be in cooler, thicker, North facing areas. Look for these feeding and bedding areas on your map in the high elevation zone. Try to identify the open feeding areas and the thicker bedding areas. Open feeding areas are immediately identifiable with the online mapping satellite views. What public roads or access points will get you close enough to enter these zones? Look over your hard copy map and your online maps. Denote vegetation type if possible.

As the rut begins in September, elk drop to slightly lower elevations than their high summer feeding grounds. This middle elevation zone is usually characterized by mountain forests well below the tree line but well above low land agricultural areas. You can still count on cow elk establishing bedding and feeding patterns. The herd bulls will be with the cows and the other satellite bulls will be on the peripheral. The satellites will also be roaming the countryside looking for open breeding opportunities. Elk like to feed in open areas and bed in thick areas slightly higher than their feeding areas. Look for open meadows on your map, aspen trees, or areas with sparse trees where understory can grow. In the Rockies, flat land and South facing slopes tend to be open areas. This is where elk will tend to feed. Bedding areas are usually within a couple miles and have a tendency to be on North facing steep slopes. Use your map to identify potential feeding and bedding locations in these middle elevation zones. Are any of these areas reachable from the public access points?

Elk Usage by Terrain on Google Maps

Migratory areas from late October to December are somewhat harder to identify and can be hit or miss. This is because you not only have to locate the travel route, but you also have to be there at the right time. The primary behavior here is travel, so you don't need to pay attention to feeding or bedding areas. Migration routes are traditional routes that follow geographic features. Scan your map for features conducive to travel. Look for pinch points. Like humans, wild game prefers to travel on the path of least resistance. These tend to be saddles, ridgelines, wooded peninsulas, and any natural feature that will funnel elk from summer zones to winter zones. Migrations generally move down in elevation but elk may be forced to move through elevated zones to reach a final lower destination. A popular method is to locate mountain saddles that game needs to travel up and over. A good method in map scouting is to locate the summer zone and winter zone and scan your map for travel routes or pinch points between them. Locating pinch points is relatively easy with a topographical map. As they are traditional, you can usually count on elk using them year after year. Which of these areas are accessible given your public access points?

Hunting late season winter zones can be feast or famine as well. Depending on when the elk migrate in, these areas may be inhabited from late October through the early summer of the following year. Elk often group up into large herds during the winter months. If there is a large herd in one area that inevitably means those elk are not occupying other areas. Elk inhabit winter zones because they have milder climates and ample feed during the winter months. They tend to be lower in elevation than surrounding areas and adjacent to ample summer feeding areas. Looking over your map, search for low valleys and vast tracts of open terrain. Hunting these zones usually requires scanning large amounts of land to find the herds. Be sure that there is ample public land at low-lying elevations if you plan to hunt during the late winter months. You will also need to ensure you have a means of accessing and covering these large tracts. Can you identify such areas on your map?

Now comes the hardest factor to predict, human pressure. Human pressure is going to vary depending on many different factors. The biggest factor is the type of tag you obtained. If it was OTC, count on a lot of pressure. If it was hard to draw, count on significantly less. I mention hunter pressure last because it overrides all other factors when it is present. Your objective is to avoid hunting pressure as much as possible. Hopefully your tag will have filtered this to some degree. If the hunting pressure where you are hunting is minimal, you can simply base your map scouting techniques on the factors listed in the paragraphs above. As this reading dedicates an entire chapter on hunting highly pressured elk, we are going to assume you are hunting an area with moderate pressure and not go into too much detail in this chapter on avoiding pressure. Looking over your map so far you likely located a few preferable hunting locations that were as close to the public roads and access areas as possible. Unfortunately, this is what the other hunters did as well. Due to fear of getting lost, difficulty of hiking, and simply not knowing any better, most hunters hunt within a one-mile radius of their vehicle. There are not many elk in this one-mile radius. You will need to mentally and physically prepare yourself to not fall victim to these characteristics. Unless there are truly no hunters at your location, forget about any potential hunting areas within a mile hike of the access roads.

A good technique to avoid hunting too close to your vehicle is to take a pencil and draw a one mile buffer line around public roads and access points on your map. Avoid hunting inside this line, that's where most other hunters will be. You should also avoid areas that have significant recreational traffic (e.g. hikers, four wheeling, camping, fishing, etc.). These recreational areas will have more traffic if they are closer to main roads, metropolitan areas, and tourist attractions (e.g. ski resorts, national parks, etc.). Another item to consider is the ease of terrain in specific locations. Hunters tend to gravitate to flat land and large open areas. This is simply because it is easy to traverse and you can see far. Even if the area looks magnificent, game quickly moves out with pressure. Avoid choosing areas simply because it looks easy to walk in, it may be highly pressured. Elk like to feed in open areas, but they don't like open areas with a lot of hunters. Open areas close to roads can resemble a pumpkin patch on opening day, lots of hunters with binoculars just looking at each other. If an area looks great, is easy to identify on the map, and is easy to reach, it will probably have many hunters. Smaller feeding and bedding areas that are harder to reach and identify will likely have less pressure. Look over your maps for public land access far from human traffic. Identify areas on the public land that are at a distance from vehicle access. Scan for areas that are not so blatantly obvious. Use logical reasoning to identify areas on your map that will have less human and hunter pressure.

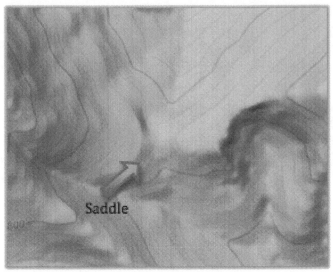

Depiction of a Saddle on Google Maps

Another popular map scouting theory often used is that of scarcity. Elk need food, water, travel routes, and cover. Depending on your hunting area, these factors will be present at varying degrees. If any of these factors are scarce, they will act as an attractant to the game. For example, on very dry years or in arid states locating water sources can be a good way to find game. In extremely open areas, look to the best cover for game. In canyons or steep mountains, perhaps a travel route such as a saddle or ridgeline will funnel the game. The higher the degree of scarcity, the more attractive the factor will be. Consider these main factors and look over your map resources for scarcity. Use climate and geography to steer your decisions. Are any of these factors accessible from public access points on your map?

The above map scouting descriptions gave generalized notions of what areas on a map will be conductive to hunting. These are areas that you have identified for further investigation. Some other general items you should keep in mind during this exercise are wind direction, road condition, and hunting logistics. The prevailing wind direction in the Rockies is usually West to Northwest, but you can check the weather in the closest town to be sure. Hunting locations should always be approached and hunted from a downwind direction; keep in mind this could require some additional footwork on your approach. Road conditions can have a positive or negative effect depending on the situation. A well-maintained road can be very attractive to hunters and outdoor enthusiasts. This can mean more pressure. However not many roads that go deep into public land are well maintained. Nearly all of them require four-wheel drive. Furthermore, just because there is a road on a map doesn't mean it's usable. Beware of roads that cross very steep terrain. These tend to be difficult to traverse and your vehicle may be worth more than the risk. Harsh weather may also make difficult roads impassable. On the other hand, difficult roads often turn back a lot of hunters. Sometimes the difficult road has less pressure. Just use good judgment as to whether it is worth the risk. It may be worthwhile to park and walk in. A quick call to the local forest service office should answer road condition questions. Hunting logistics is a non-hunting factor to be considered throughout your hunt. Depending on where you plan to find lodging, camp, or access general resources, may have a bearing on where you hunt. Keep in mind that the areas that are more convenient tend to have more hunters.

If I have no experience hunting in a unit, I try to identify at least three to five locations that I plan to scout in person before the hunt. I pinpoint these locations through mapping resources and the processes described above. This should be your goal as well. Make sure you have multiple locations identified from your maps. Hunt planning is not complete at this phase. These are simply the areas that will be investigated further. Too many hunters put all their eggs into one basket only to find that the game is not there or that there are too many hunters in the one spot they planned on hunting. You should always have a plan B and C location and you will need to confirm the game usage in each through the next few discussed resources.

The mapping resource is one of the top resources in your arsenal. Veteran western hunters spend countless hours pouring over maps. It may seem difficult at first, but the more time you spend honing in on a unit, the better off you will be when you arrive. Obtain a quality map and spend a good deal of time educating yourself on the unit and possible hunting locations. Utilize online mapping to refine your plan.

6. State Employees and Forest Service Employees

Often the individuals who work in the area have the best knowledge of it. Not only do state and federal employees work in hunting areas, it is their job to monitor the herds and habitat. Contacting state and federal officials for information is a seldom used resource. It can be used in the tag-planning phase, but more often than not is better utilized during the hunt-planning phase.

Lets cover tag planning first. State officials can provide very useful information regarding specific application procedures. Most states even have individuals in positions specifically for answering application and drawing questions. Contact information is usually listed on both the state wildlife website and within the hunting regulations. Asking generic questions about the best hunting areas will produce feedback, but often application oriented personnel do not have statewide game backgrounds. Their positions are usually customer service oriented. The biologists and unit game managers are the ones that are intimately familiar with game habits. But these individuals are usually not included in application personnel and are better utilized after you have a tag in hand. In any case, your questions regarding the best hunting units are better answered and supported by the statistical data on the state wildlife website. Application service magazines also offer it in a very organized and digestible manner. The information to be taken from state and federal employees relates to application procedures or specific unit hunt planning, which we will now dive into.

Hunt planning resources have no definite order of precedence. In fact, most of the information to be gathered is so interrelated that it must be compared and combined with other information sources. Contacting state and federal employees falls within this conglomeration. In the hunt-planning phase, you are seeking information specific to hunting units or areas within a unit. Certain state and federal employees have extensive experience in specific units or with specific species. These are the biologists and game managers. Lets talk about a few different reasons and situations where it is helpful to contact these individuals.

Deep in the world of western hunting are those hunters who seek the largest trophies and settle for nothing less. As this book is more directed toward the common hunter, we will not spend a great deal of time on the monsters only subject. Nevertheless, for trophy hunters the state agency biologists are indispensable. These are the individuals who can inform hunters of the exact trophy potential within an area, for that specific year, and recommended locations to find these genetics. This can be very helpful in terms of expectations and hunt planning. The state wildlife website should provide a contact information page that gives general phone numbers as well as regional office phone numbers. Regions are usually large areas within a state that encompass multiple hunting units. Contact either the general number or regional office and identify the type of information you are seeking. This process is fairly common and the state employees should be able to put you in touch with the correct individuals. Be prepared with the specific questions you wish to have answered.

Most western hunters are happy with mature bucks and bulls. For these individuals, seeking the knowledge of state and federal employees can be very helpful too, as they can inform you on game habits. The state and federal employees to be contacted are those that work within the region or unit you wish to scout and hunt. Similar to map scouting, you are trying to identify multiple locations to scout first hand and to hunt in. These employees can match game hot spots to map locations. They can also provide hunting pressure movements, migratory information, wintering areas, and sync the time of year to elevation movements. Contact the regional wildlife managers in the locations you wish to hunt. The contact information should be available on the state website, or the general phone number can be called to ask for the contact information of the specific individuals or offices to call. You should also search for Forest Service or BLM offices that service the unit you are researching. State parks can also provide recommendations, both within their park and in the surrounding areas. Any employees that work directly with the habitat and game in the area will have hands on knowledge of game movement. Be prepared to make a few phone calls to see what information you can gather, and don't get deterred if some of your calls are not fruitful. If you can step foot into these office locations and speak to these individuals in person, it is certainly your best option, especially if you have a map in hand to converse over specific locations.

When speaking with these individuals, you should already have an idea as to how you want the conversation to go. Begin by identifying yourself and your targeted information. State your unit, weapon, and the dates you will be hunting. Don't forget to mention how thankful you are that they are willing to help you. Your first and most important question is simple. What locations or areas would you recommend to hunt in? Ask about the hunter pressure in the area. Ask if there is a general movement of game when pressured. Ask about the elevations the game will be inhabiting, when they will be rutting, where migration zones are, and where the winter habitat is. If you already have some areas in mind, ask if these areas are advisable to hunt in. Often these individuals will provide general recommendations based on geographical features rather than specific hunting locations. For instance, they may recommend an area South of a specific mountain peak or a large drainage accessed by a specific road. They may only reference a general part of the unit, such as the northern half. Be sure to have your map in hand during these discussions. Write down the areas that are recommended. The information offered usually is not extremely specific, but it can be extremely helpful. Telling you to concentrate on a specific elevation or area within a unit zeros in your hunting options. During this process also bear in mind that these employees are giving this information out of kindness. They are not required to give you hunting recommendations. Be sure to remain humble and express gratitude for any information revealed.

Advice obtained from employees who work in the area is priceless. If you have followed all the resource recommendations so far, you should start to narrow down what areas you wish to hunt in. Between the map scouting and employee data, you should have a strong base of knowledge to build upon with the remaining resources.

7. Experienced Hunters

Similar to state and federal employees, there are many hunters willing to give advice on western hunting and specific hunting units. It can be extremely useful if it is trustworthy but very misleading if it does not come from a trustworthy source. For this reason I often find myself stating why this information should not be followed rather than why it should be followed. The list of resources is ordered in terms of timing rather than significance. If the list were based on significance, this would undoubtedly be last. Even so, it deserves adequate attention given its usefulness if it comes from a trustworthy source.

Seeking this type of information can be difficult. It isn't retrievable at your discretion as the other resources are. This resource requires a live person to actively give advice based on personal experience. The advice itself also takes many forms. It can be either general or specific. It may reference tag planning or hunt planning. But as hunt planning is more than adequately covered by unbiased state statistics and application service magazines, I recommend you leave your tag decisions to the objective research. The objective statistics do not recommend specific hunting locations within units though. For this reason, it is always worth lending an ear to anyone who wishes to provide hunting advice. Before taking it for gospel, consider the source. Is this a trusted friend or relative? Does the individual have first hand experience in a unit? Or is it third hand? Absorb as much of it as you can, but keep in mind that it is very subjective in nature.

So how does one find experienced hunters from your unit to speak with? We can certainly list a few sources, but often this information comes from seizing chance opportunities. If you are lucky, a close friend or relative has experience hunting an area that they can share. Maybe they can recommended a hunting area or vouch for an area you are researching. Maybe they can recommend an area to avoid, which can be just as useful. Accessing trustworthy advice from hunters you do not know is somewhat more difficult. It does become significantly more trustworthy the closer you are to the unit you are examining though. I have bumped into numerous hunters while scouting, hunting, fishing, camping, or simply being in units I wish to hunt in. I have also bumped into many state and federal employees in this manner. You can always stop by the local outdoor store, butcher shop, taxidermist, or outfitter to see if anyone is willing to provide insight. It certainly helps if you provide a mutually beneficial relationship. For instance, if you are purchasing a map or fishing license from an outdoor store the owner may be more responsive to your questions. When you are actually on a western hunt, you usually run into other hunters along the roadside, when passing their camps, or even in the field. I have found that the friendlier I am, the friendlier they are. I openly share information about what game I have seen and usually let them know the general area I am focusing on. Often they share the same information. You may be surprised how friendly westerners are on public hunting land. Obviously you should remain humble in your inquiries, but general questions should retrieve useful advice. Focus on the same questions we covered in the state and federal employee resource. These are the recommended area, pressure, game movement, active elevation, and rutting questions.

If you don't know anyone who has hunted your unit and you can't travel there to inquire with locals, there are still a few options. In fact, we already covered a few in previous resources. Previous hunters often comment on the online forums and blogs mentioned in the Internet search resource. Inquiring on these websites will usually foster responses. But take these with a grain of salt. State and federal employees mentioned in the previous resource usually have extensive hunting experience in the area as well. And of course there is always the option that comes with a price, application services.

Application Service magazines often include first hand advice on specific units and where to hunt within those units as part of their service package. This may come in the form of magazine articles, email question and answer, or it may require a direct phone call. Some of these organizations will even provide the contact information of hunters that drew tags in specific units in prior years. Thus creating a network of useful hunting information. You can imagine how priceless this information can be. If interested, inquire with these service organizations to see if this is offered as part of their package.

Advice from previous hunters can be quite valuable if from a trustworthy source. At the end of the day, this type of information is classified as "listeners beware." Not so surprising is the fact that most first time western hunters depend almost entirely on this information to plan their hunts. Maybe someone's friend told your hunting group of a secret location in a mountain range that no one hunts. The reality is, not many areas are secret. The ones that are secret remain so because no one is talking about them, especially from states away. The statistics will show dependable success and hunter pressure in a given unit. Experienced hunter advice can provide details but should be confirmed as reliable before depended upon.

8. Hunting Books and Videos

Many notable authors and contemporary hunters have published books and DVDs containing valuable information on western hunting. Case in point, you're reading one right now. Numerous books and DVDs exist for all western species to be hunted. These cover western hunting from A to Z. The higher-level concepts shed some light on tag planning concepts. These themes include weather, weapon types, terrain, etc., but the bulk of the information is in reference to hunting tactics or actual hunts. The themes include scouting, glassing, stalking, driving, calling, personal experiences, etc. This is a very useful resource in learning different hunting tactics. Find a book on elk hunting that does well in describing the different tactics and read and reread such tactics. Use videos to learn about calling, as the audio recording is needed to perfect your skills. CD's can also be useful when learning to call. Tactics are more correlated with hunt planning. As most of the information is not in direct relation to your specific tag or unit, the information gained is somewhat independent from your tag planning processes. Meaning this valuable resource is not time sensitive and can be performed at your leisure without regard to application dates, map reading, Internet searches, or phone calls.

We should also recognize that many video productions are purely for entertainment and are not meant to be educational. This is not the type of video recommended in this text. Entertainment is just entertainment, and it often gives the wrong message. Real western hunting is not as shown on outdoor television shows. Educational programs and DVDs meant to teach hunters facts about elk, terrain, and offer tips and tactics are useful. These are the types of DVDs you should focus on if you wish to gain knowledge in western hunting. Given the thin line between entertainment and education DVDs, how-to hunting books are a much better information source than television shows.

For many hunters, reading books and watching videos dedicated to western hunting happens in the background. Perhaps you decide to pick up an elk-hunting book simply out of curiosity. Maybe a looming western hunt is on the horizon and you wish to gain a better understanding of your trip. Books are also used as reference guides to refer back to just before or during hunting seasons. Such literature can offer valuable tactical knowledge.

For planning purposes, the information offered is somewhat general. It is certainly recommended to pick up a highly rated western hunting book or how-to DVD in your spare time before your hunt. While reading or watching, try to soak in the bigger themes related to tag planning. It will help you decide what type of terrain you wish to hunt in, when you wish to hunt, and how you would like to hunt. Much of this literature is also quite educational on game characteristics and habits. The more you know about the animal you wish to pursue, the better decisions you will make while hunting. The most valuable information to gain is in regard to hunting tactics. Specific hunting techniques are described in detail. This is the knowledge you will need while actually hunting. It may also come in very handy when scouting. Given the type of hunting terrain and animal behavior on your hunt, you will need to choose what the best-hunting tactics are. For example, open terrain is more conducive to glassing and stand hunting. Thick terrain may be better for still-hunting. Rutting animals may be better pursued through calling. All scenarios are adequately covered. This knowledge is then matched with your hunting area. As hunting tactic information is well covered in most western hunting books, we will not dive into it for hunt planning purposes.

Hunting books and informational DVDs build your base of knowledge and guide your actions while in the field. As valuable as they are, they fail to specifically help you in researching units, choosing tags, or reading maps. That is the type of information needed when planning a hunt. Use the knowledge you gain with this resource to assist you when conducting your hunt.

9. Scouting

The research resources described thus far have all taken place well in advance of the hunting season. Additionally, most only require an Internet connection. Scouting is the one pre-hunt exception. It requires a bit more time and effort. This resource pertains directly to hunt planning. Sometimes one may scout an area before they decide to put in for a tag, but this is not the norm for non-resident hunters. Statistical data should serve that purpose. Scouting should take place after you have received your tag and followed through with the many available resources to narrow down your targeted hunting locations. Scouting is the most inconvenient resource, as it requires you to travel to your hunting area before the season begins. For logistical reasons, many hunters simply cannot allocate the time and money to set up a trip merely for scouting. This is understandable, but the benefits of scouting are immense. If at all possible, a hunter should make an effort to scout before they embark on a western hunt.

Your scouting efforts preferably should take place when game is in the area. This means you should scout close to the time of year you will be hunting. However, you must take all precautions not to scare game out of the area while scouting. Sometimes the best time to scout depends on the type of terrain you are hunting. If it is possible to scout using long-range tactics, usually meaning glassing open terrain, it is best to scout in the days just before your hunt begins. If your hunting area is too thick and you cannot scout using long-range tactics, I recommend scouting in advance of the season so you do not spook game. Scouting well in advance of the season eliminates the need long-range techniques, but game moves around a bit and it doesn't guarantee game will be there on opening day. For this reason, the ideal method is to scout both in advance and in the days just before the season too. I will often spend a weekend during the summer scouting, and then show up a couple days before the season begins to locate game. Using this method I can get very up close and personal with the terrain ahead of time and also locate game immediately before the season starts. But lets face it, unless you live somewhat close by, this method is not going to be feasible. If you can only take one trip, I would recommend showing up a few days before the season starts and being very careful to use long range tactics and not spook game. If you have a long season to hunt, such as many of the western archery seasons, you may simply be able to allocate more time to your trip and get to know the area over a longer period of hunting. In this situation, the first few days of your hunt are a combination of scouting and hunting together.

Long Range Scouting, Colorado

All of your hunt planning thus far has been in an effort to narrow down your hunting location options. If you have followed the advice in this reading, you should have three to five locations in mind within your unit. These locations should be noted on your map. In scouting, you actually show up to these locations to gain first hand knowledge of the area. Most hunters assume scouting is merely walking an area looking for animals and sign. While very important, this is too narrow a focus.

Scouting should begin with a broad focus. When I arrive to a unit the first thing I focus on is covering as much terrain as I can. All of your efforts so far have been from a distance. Now that you can actually see and travel through your unit, the information to be gained is much more accurate. I begin by driving all around the unit through the areas and roads I located on the map. I do not simply drive up to the three to five locations I have pinpointed; I drive through and around all the public land and access points. I drive past my pinpointed locations to see them from different vantage points and to see what surrounds them. This gives you a good idea of the access, the condition of the roads, and what the terrain looks like in person. Some of your locations will inevitably look much better than others. Maybe an area you had originally crossed off your list looks enticing. Maybe an area you thought would be your number one choice has multiple houses nearby or seems like too popular an access point. Maybe an access road is inaccessible due to private land. Perhaps the vegetation is too dense in one area or the terrain too steep. At this point you may need to reassess your target locations. Maybe you can find a new one or the three to five you have in mind turns into two. In any case, driving all around your unit and your target locations gives you a good feel for the terrain.

After a thorough vehicle tour of the area you should reassess and begin to hike and scout your targeted locations. Throughout this process you will be comparing each location against one another to determine which seems best. I recommend focusing on the top three locations that look best after you have driven around the unit. Other areas should not be forgotten altogether, but scouting more than three locations will take a significant amount of time. If time is no issue, scout as many as possible. From a practical sense, narrowing your focus to the top three will give you ample time to scout. If none of these three seem promising, you can always fall back to the others.

So how does one scout the specific areas you wish to hunt? To begin, use a logical approach to finding entry areas that will have less human and hunter traffic. Recall the lessons learned in the map scouting section. Your targeted entry point or parking location should avoid busy trailheads, high traffic recreation areas, and very easy to access land. If a location is so convenient that it seems a lot of hunters will be there, they will be. That doesn't mean you need to avoid an area completely, simply distance yourself a few miles from the high traffic area. A good method to do so is to park along forest roads rather than at their busy trailheads. Hunters tend to gravitate to the very end of forest roads assuming this will get them the farthest into the backcountry. It does, but it bypasses a lot of land and starts you off with many other hunters. Try to avoid camping areas or all terrain vehicle (ATV) trails. Wilderness areas limit vehicle transportation and can often offer more solitude. Areas with fewer roads usually offer more solitude once you distance yourself from the few roads. If an area does not allow overnight camping or parking, it likely will have less people. Use common sense to avoid the pressured areas and access points. Remember you will likely be hunting at a distance from your vehicle. The further you are from hunters and human traffic the more game there will be. Keep in mind that game avoids human pressure, not necessarily human existence. Sometimes pressure does not equate to hiking as far as you can, but rather just finding an area others bypass. For example, on a recent Wyoming hunt my brother and I noticed a herd of elk crossing a road less than a mile into the National Forest from the highway. We decided to spend the morning hunting the area and quickly realized that we had it all to ourselves. Elk were plentiful and the area was overlooked by hunters simply because it was so close to the main highway. These are the types unpressured pockets you can sometimes find. Reference the locations you have targeted on your map and find a suitable access point that avoids human pressure as much as possible. After finding your parking location, it's time to burn some boot rubber.

Given the terrain and season you are hunting, you should be focusing on one of the animal behavioral characteristics as discussed earlier. Employ subtle scouting methods and try to avoid pushing any game. Utilize long-range glassing during the active game hours (i.e. morning and evening). Long-range scouting is somewhat self-explanatory. Locate glassing points, usually at high points – but really anywhere that affords a good view where you can use optics to view the game at a distance while it is traveling or feeding. If the terrain does not afford long range scouting, only access the areas you wish to hunt if you can do so without spooking the game. Listen for elk vocalization. Try to predict the game habits and general movements. This means looking for feeding, bedding, and the travel routes between. Identify ambush points or a manageable plan to get within striking distance. Access feeding and watering areas to look for sign when the game is not present. Only when the game is not present should you physically enter the exact areas the game is using. This is either well in advance of the season or midday.

The first goal in scouting is to ensure the terrain is used for the purpose or behavior you are targeting it for. For example, if it is a feeding area you are targeting, ensure that there is ample food. For elk, this usually means plenty of open grass. The process is similar for bedding areas, pinch points, travel corridors, wintering areas, etc. Ensure the terrain you are targeting contains the physical traits needed for this purpose. Such characteristics are easily recognized. The question is usually whether the elk are using it, rather than if it has the right characteristics. There is a lot of terrain out West, so the game has choices. After ensuring the area has the correct characteristics, you will need to ensure the game is using your area by locating fresh sign. At this point, it is worth reiterating the fact that western game is often migratory and uses different areas for different times of the year. Therefore just because you find animal sign in an area doesn't mean the game uses it during your hunting season. You should have already factored this into your scouting efforts, but it is worth mentioning again. Ensure that your elevation and target areas match the game characteristics at that time of year. This is why scouting near your hunting season is helpful, because it is much easier look for fresh sign.

Animal sign comes in a few different forms. The best form is the animal itself. Once again, this is why it is best to scout when the game is actually in the area. Cover the terrain as if you are actually hunting. Move slowly and try the techniques you plan to use while hunting. Keep the wind in your favor. Stalk, glass, and remember to be as discreet as possible as you take in your surroundings. This will increase your chances of seeing game and decrease your chances of spooking it. Seeing game is definitely the best form of sign as you can watch the animal movements and pattern their behavior. Too often hunters blow game out of an area when scouting. If you scout well in advance of the season this will not matter as much, but it is always better to tread as lightly as you can keep the game comfortable in the area.

Work the land very slowly and look for any form of animal sign. Obviously the more sign you come across the better the area is. The common forms of elk sign are tracks, trails, droppings, rubs, and wallows. Keep in mind that many different animal species use the terrain out West. You will need to distinguish different sign by species. With a trained eye, one can do so fairly easily. Antelope, sheep, goat, and bear sign tends to either be in different terrain or is easily differentiated from elk sign, so we will not go over them in depth. Moose and deer inhabit the same terrain and have similar sign. Moose tend to be few and far between with much larger tracks and droppings, so confusion is not much of an issue. Their tracks are about five or six inches in length and much more narrow than those of elk. Mule deer droppings and tracks are similar in size and shape to whitetail deer. Their tracks are usually about three inches in length and small all around. Size is your main differential between elk, moose, and deer sign. Sometimes domestic cattle and sheep use the same ground elk inhabit. Open range grazing is practiced on public land throughout the West. Cattle tracks can be somewhat confusing with elk tracks. Like moose, cattle tracks are much larger thank elk. Cattle also tend to stick to areas close to the roads and access points. The cattle themselves are often present in these areas as well. Before scouting, familiarize yourself with pictures of the tracks and droppings of the different western species.

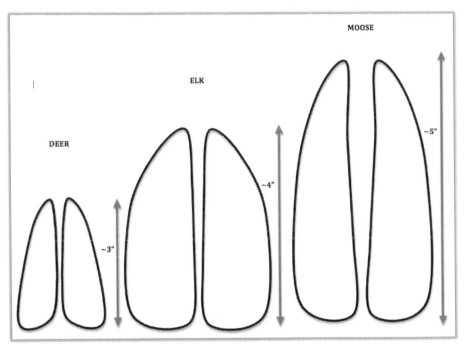

Elk Track Differentiation

Elk sign is easily recognized. Elk are gregarious by nature and tend to live in groups and herds. Herds leave considerable sign when they move through areas. Lets talk about the different forms of sign you should be looking for.

Elk tracks tell you where elk have been. This gives you a good idea of where they will be in the future. The more tracks, the better the area. Tracks can lead to trails or be disbursed through the woods and parks. Whatever the case, they give a good indication of how often elk use the area. More tracks mean more usage. Elk tracks are about the size of a fist or around four inches long. They are distinctively heart shaped. If you find an area with a significant amount of tracks, use the context information to predict why the elk are using the area. Maybe it is leading to a trail or maybe you are in a feeding area. Check to see how fresh the tracks are. Are the edges of the track crisp and distinctly shaped or do the tracks look dull and deformed? Elk sign may remain in an area for years. Softer ground is usually better for aging tracks (e.g. mud, sand, snow).

The fresher the tracks are, the better. Fresh tracks mean elk are currently using the area. Take note to how much sign is in the area, you will be comparing this to other locations during your efforts. As you find hot spots, you will begin to formulate your hunting tactics according to the amount of sign and the behavioral characteristics.

Game trails are easily recognized. They are formed by converging tracks on commonly travelled routes through the mountains and parks. They may be faint or well dug in. The more frequent a trail is used the less vegetation will be present on it. Frequently used trails look like miniature dirt roads through the woods. When you find trails in the woods note the direction they travel. Sometimes they link feeding and bedding sites. They may simply follow the path of least resistance crossing terrain, such as up and over saddles or on ridgelines. Whatever their purpose, they tend to be used as highways through the wilderness. Walk along these to get a better idea of why elk are using them. Look closely at the trail to ensure it is covered with elk tracks. Look even closer to see if you can tell how fresh the tracks are. The fresher the sign is the better. As with all forms of sign, look for areas with more of it for hot spots. Areas with a lot of trails, heavily used trails, or areas where trails intersect are good areas to hunt.

Elk droppings are often found in conjunction with trails and tracks. Elk droppings are larger than deer droppings in both length and size. They take either pellet shape or are in a clumplike mass. This is usually an indication of what they have eaten. Pellet form is more common, but rich diets of mostly grasses will be clumplike. Sometimes the droppings will be a mixture of the two. The common hunter-lore is that bulls tend to leave distinct piles while cows tend to spread out their droppings. While helpful, don't base all your efforts on this idea. Once again, this form of sign can remain in an area for years. Freshness indicates whether the area is currently in use or not. Droppings deposited recently will still be soft and moist. The moister they are, the fresher they are. If they are warm, they are very fresh. Yes, checking their temperature requires you to touch them. How bad do you want that bull?

Many hunters only check temperature when they are actually hunting. Like the previous signs, more is better. Use the surrounding clues to determine why and how often elk use an area. Consider hunting in areas with large amounts of droppings.

Elk Droppings

Rutting animals leave distinct signs as well. For elk, this comes in the form of rubs and wallows. Rubs follow the same concept as deer. Elk rub trees with their antlers before and during the rut. This removes bark, breaks branches, and recognizably disrupts the appearance of the tree. The difference between a deer and elk rub is the size. Elk have much larger bodies and antlers. As they are larger creatures, they tend to rub on larger trees. The antlers extend very high into the air, so the rubs may extend very high on the tree as their antlers scrape the trunk and break branches. Sometimes you can get an indication of animal size based on the rub size. A mature elk can stand five feet at the shoulder, and the antlers another three to five feet above them when rubbing. This gives you an idea of possible rub height. The larger the tree and rub; the larger the animal. Rubs indicate where rutting activity has taken place in your area. Multiple rubs tend to string through the woods on a line. This can give you an idea of a route travelled by a bull. You should also be able to quickly tell if a rub is fresh by fine bark shavings both still attached to the tree and on the ground. The rubbed tree may also be moist, have sap protruding, or show green bark layers at the edges. As always, more rubs indicate a better area. Look to areas with multiple rubs if you intend to hunt the rut.

Elk wallows are a very unique phenomenon in big game hunting. Essentially these are slightly depressed muddy puddles about the size of a double bed. They occur in secluded areas where small water deposits create puddle-like depressions. Water sources may be small streams, springs, or runoff that meanders into puddles. Elk roll around in these wallows for a few reasons, but mostly for breeding purposes. Bull elk will urinate and deposit droppings in the wallow then roll through to cover themselves in scent. Cow elk may be drawn to the scent and use the wallow as well, but for the most part these wallows are bull magnets. They are easily recognized and should have numerous fresh tracks in and surrounding the depression. They also have considerable droppings in them and a foul smell when active. If it is not breeding season, the wallow will still be easily recognized, but the sign will not be fresh. Wallows are one of the few times elk hunters will sit still and stand hunt. Multiple bulls may consistently visit an active wallow during the rut. If you find an area with a few wallows or one with considerable sign, plan on making a trip there during the breeding season. Locating wallows can be difficult. Following slight water sources is a good tactic. Often wallows are stumbled upon by chance. Whatever the case, be sure to mark them on your map or GPS. Elk tend to use them more during dry conditions, in the evenings, and during the earlier phase of the rut.

The next few signs we will cover are somewhat harder to locate but can be very helpful. The first is subtle signs left from grazing. This is often referred to as cropping. Feeding areas that are consistently used may appear as though spots have been hit with a weed whacker. The appearance of grass and forbs snipped off at their base is often the product of animal grazing. Elk tend to be the culprits of this sign as they predominately eat grasses in open areas. As you pass through possible feeding areas (e.g. parks, South facing slopes and ridgelines, marshes) pay close attention to the grasses and plants. It may be subtle, but check to see if they are cropped. Areas used heavily for feeding will be more noticeable. If you find this, it is a very strong sign that elk are using an area for feeding. Though you likely will not be scouting in the winter, feeding is very apparent when snows cover the ground as elk sweep snow out of the way with their hooves or head to reach food.

Lush Aspen Grove, Colorado

Aspen forests cover many areas throughout the Rockies. These deciduous trees create prime wildlife habitat. This is primarily because more sunlight reaches the ground and more understory grows. Aspen tree forests should be located and targeted as feeding areas. Look for grass cropping in these areas as well. Elk also dine on the bark of aspen trees. As you walk through these forests look for rigid scrapes on the trees around the head height of a standing elk. These marks are very apparent on the white bark of aspen trees. Fresh tooth marks indicate elk are feeding in the area. As with all sign, the more cropping and aspen scrapes the better. Targeting aspen areas as a whole is a good idea, those with chewed bark provide solid evidence.

Another useful sign is shed antlers. But these are few and far between. They also fall in the winter months so they likely will not be at the higher elevations. Low lying winter areas will hold the bulk of sheds. If you plan to hunt late season, they are a good indicator of where the elk will be. These also provide assurance of antler quality and bull health in an area. We should note that shed collecting is a popular hobby in itself. That being so, many people embark on shed collecting trips each year to wintering hot spots. As soon as antlers fall many are quickly collected. If you plan to hunt a wintering area, the best time to scout is during that time of year. Perhaps a shed collecting trip is something you will enjoy as well. Known wintering areas are sometimes closed from human interaction so as not to disturb vulnerable wintering or calving elk. Check the regulations in an area before showing up and finding a locked gate.

Oddly enough, you can sometimes follow your nose to elk. Many hunters have a hard time believing this until they personally encounter the smell of elk or moose. Elk have a very musky smell, especially during the rut. I often liken their smell to a cattle barn. When in close proximity to upwind elk, you often can smell them. As you hike your hunting areas, be mindful of any musky animal or cattle like smells you come across, you may be very close to elk. I have mistakenly followed my nose to moose though. In any case, you can count on being very close to game if you can smell them.

Lastly, we will touch on elk vocalizations. As gregarious creatures, elk frequently communicate. Bull elk bugle during the rut, and all elk communicate through mews and chirps year round. Some refer to this as herd talk. Hunters often hear elk long before they see them. When scouting, keep a stout ear for any elk vocalizations. Bugles can be heard from a very long distance. If you are scouting or hunting during the rut, bugles are one of the best mechanisms to locate bulls. Listen for bugles in the morning, evening, and throughout the night. The more distinctly different bugles you hear the more bulls are in the area. I have often noticed that elk bugles are closer than they sound. You can even pattern bull movements through their bugles. Cows communicate with herd talk. Through all the elk literature I have come across, I have never found it easy to draw a connection to an elk mew through its formal spelling. The common spelling of an elk mew is something like "eeeuuuuhh." For this reason, you should search for online recordings to familiarize yourself with the live sounds of elk. Though herd talk isn't near as loud as a bugle, it happens all year long and is often constant in large herds. When in the elk woods, diligently listen for any elk communication. It will often redirect your movements and lead you to elk. It can also be useful in pinpointing elk while stalking them. Familiarize yourself with the common sounds of elk. Videos and audio CD's specifically on this topic are very helpful. As you scout, you can even do a bit of calling to possibly communicate with elk in the area.

Scouting for elk follows the main research theme of narrowing down your hunting options. After driving your area, locating preferable entry points, glassing, walking the area as if you are hunting, and looking for the tell tale signs of game, you should have discovered which of your three top areas seem the most promising. At this point you can rank them and decide which one will be your first choice hunting spot. If you were scouting well in advance of the season, you should still show up a few days early to confirm elk are still in the area. Locate fresh sign and find the spot you will focus your efforts on opening day. If you could only show up a few days before your hunt, you should still follow the same procedures outlined in this chapter. You just have to be a bit more careful not to spook game.

While performing your scouting, search until you locate fresh sign. If there is not fresh sign, elk are not in the area. If elk are not in the area, you shouldn't be either. Too many hunters show up to one spot and will not move even if elk sign is not present. If elk are not there, move to a different area. This is why you should target multiple locations. It is not uncommon to have to fall back to a plan B or C location. Keep moving until you find the area with fresh sign. Do not waste your time if elk are not present. You will find them if you keep looking, you just may have to move around a bit. That could mean different elevations or possibly moving a few miles to an undisturbed area.

If you have followed all of the research advice thus far, you have now completed just about all you can before embarking on your hunt. Hopefully your pre-scouting research was confirmed with plenty of sign and game in your hunting locations. Formulate your plan based on the evidence you found, the information you have gathered, and logical planning. Good luck hunting!

10. Hunting

It seems counterintuitive that hunting is considered a research resource. All resources discussed so far have been preparing one for the hunt, so how can the hunt itself be a resource? The hunt is a research resource because it provides the most hands on knowledge of all. Hunters should not think of a western hunt as a repetitive process wherein they wait for game to eventually turn up. Elk are not as habitual as whitetail deer. More time logged will not ensure success. A western hunter needs to adapt to the animal movements and continuously change tactics based on success and failure. Western animals cover large distances and move in and out of areas. So do successful western hunters.

You will log more time on the ground in your unit while hunting than with any other resource. Experience is not speculation. You are physically witnessing how the game is or is not using an area. This should guide your actions during your hunt and possibly for future hunts. Pattern the animals based on their movements. Formulate short-term plans to utilize the best hunting tactic to get close enough for a shot. This may require various forms of hunting. For example, you may still-hunt your way to a large overlook and then glass upon arrival. Or you may chase bugles and call in the morning while hiking to a wallow for a stand hunt that evening. These are educated strategies that are directly based on how the game is using your area. If your plans are not bearing fruit, adjust and reformulate your plans.

One of the best pieces of information to be gained from the actual hunt is the hunter pressure in the area. The statistics give general notions and speaking with experienced hunters may have shed some light, but you will not know for sure until you show up to your locations and see how hunters use the unit and where they go in the unit. There is much knowledge to be gained just from the amount of camps and vehicles parked along roads and trailheads. Avoiding hunter pressure is a necessity. Over the years I have had to adapt numerous strategies because too many hunters had the same plan I had. The hunting public knows many of the top hunting areas. Many hunters who scouted just as you did found the areas you located. During your hunt you should adapt your strategies to avoid the pressured areas. If you show up to your first choice location to find it choked with trucks and orange vests, check out your second choice. Try to gain a feel for the areas hunters gravitate to. Learning how an area gets pressured is valuable knowledge. This can come in very handy for your current and future hunts. It will have a bearing on the game movements, indicate areas to avoid, and inevitably indicate which areas to target. If there is too much pressure in an area, move elsewhere.

The idea of strategy adaptation has been mentioned a few times. Hunting in your unit will give you first hand experience with game movements, hunter pressure, and personal failures and successes. This information should continuously transform your strategies. If a strategy, plan, or tactic is working, continue with it until it dries up. If the area is abundant with game, continue hunting there. If the area is void of game, do not assume you just need to wait it out. The nature of western game is nomadic. Elk get pressured each year and have their own strategies to avoid hunters. If an area dries up, move to your next location. Continuously look for fresh sign. If your next area is just as void, go to your third area. Your scouting and research should have provided back up plans. Don't hesitate to use them.

Hunting has a profound way of being both amazing and disappointing. The knowledge you gain from your hunt will only improve you as a hunter. It will help in the short-term during your current hunt and give you insight into future hunts. The information gained during your actual hunt is the best knowledge to be gained during the entire research process. Soak in as much information as you can and adapt your strategy accordingly.

The following example will give you a good idea as to how strategy adaptation can lead to success. On a recent Arizona hunt I followed all the advice outlined in the preceding resources. I did all my homework and showed up to the unit a few days ahead of time to scout for game. However all the target locations from my maps, conversations, and research were not producing results. I had thoroughly glassed and scouted four locations that looked great and were recommended by state officials and previous hunters. Everything was there: food, water, trails, bedding areas, saddles, escape routes, everything except for fresh sign and elk. In my days of scouting I spoke with a few other hunters who had also yet to see any elk. They were hoping that elk would soon show up due to pressure or for other unknown reasons. As you may have guessed, my opening morning came and went without an elk sighting. I had been in the unit three days without seeing an elk. I decided I wasn't going to wait for elk to magically appear like the other hunters. Still sitting on my morning glassing point, I opened my map, devised a plan, and hiked three miles back to camp. By 2:00PM on opening day I had packed camp and was off to a different part of the unit. The next paragraph describes my thought process.

The late October weather was unseasonably warm. In addition, a hunting camp I bumped into the previous day informed me that a cow only rifle hunt had preceded the bull rifle hunt this year. I was dealing with heat and pressure. Given the situation, I knew my next move would have to be higher in elevation (where it is cooler) and to avoid pressure. Pondering my next move, I recalled reading online that an area of the unit consistently receives less pressure. In looking at that area on the map, it was obvious why. The referenced location was a narrow panhandle section of the unit bordered by an interstate on one side and a large canyon system on the other. There weren't many roads and it was laced with meandering finger canyons jutting towards the interstate. The geography was simply undesirable and difficult to hunt. It was also higher in elevation. I studied the map and came up with my Plan E. Hiking back to the truck, packing camp, and driving the ten or so miles to the new area took some time, but it was better than sitting in an area that was void of elk. As I left my camp I passed another hunter on the forest service road. Stopping to chat, I mentioned that I had not seen anything yet and told him that I was relocating. He seemed puzzled by this. He had not seen any elk either, but he was going to remain anyway and keep hunting in hopes of elk showing.

Upon arrival at the new location it was apparent that the only possible roadside camping locations were in sight of a busy interstate. This in itself was enough to keep hunters away, but elk don't mind the sounds of a highway. After parking and hiking in a mile or so, I came to the first canyon. It was deep enough to keep anyone from crossing it. I just knew the game had to be thick on the other side. That evening I only saw one elk, but it was enough to motivate me to find a way across that canyon in the morning. I poured over the contour lines of my map that night and found what looked to be a mild way across. First light the next morning found me glassing the ravine. Within twenty minutes I found a way over that was surprisingly easy. As I had guessed, fresh sign was immediately abundant on the other side. I proceeded to hunt and scout all day long. That evening I found a bull in my scope, and it turned out to be the last day of my hunt. Relocating and pushing until I found fresh sign was the key. I had not found elk until the fifth spot I scouted. As I packed the elk out the next day, I wondered if the hunters in the first area were still waiting for elk to show up.

Hunting is the best way to learn your hunting area. Elk move around a lot. You should too until you locate them. Always have a back up plan and do not hesitate to use it. The more time you spend in a unit, the more you will hone your tactics and learn how the game uses the area. This can come in especially handy if you plan to return for future hunts. Use logic and react to situational pressure to guide your actions.

Chapter 9 - High Pressure Tags

Sometimes the lure of an easy to obtain tag is too much to resist. We can go over the reasons to avoid high-pressure tags again and again, but we all inevitably purchase one from time to time. These tags simply have too much hunter pressure. Rather than beating a dead horse, lets accept the fact that we may end up with one from time to time and discuss a few tips and tactics when hunting with high pressure tags.

A high-pressure tag is any tag that allows a lot of hunters to access an area at the same time. These tags may be OTC, easy to draw, or a combination of separate species hunts that take place at the same time. OTC tags are almost always highly pressured. Very easy to draw tags are usually less pressured than OTC tags, but can often be classified as high pressure as well. Some areas may issue an abundance of cow tags and only a few hard to draw bull tags. Even though the bull tag was difficult to draw, the area is high pressure because of the amount of hunters in the woods chasing cows. In addition, specific areas can be highly pressured simply because of the ease of access. For instance, major trailheads near towns and cities can get pressured even when the tag is somewhat difficult to obtain. This is because many hunters simply do not know where to go and stack up at the same points.

So the question is, what techniques can you use to increase your harvest success with high-pressure tags? The short answer is simple: avoid as much hunter pressure as possible. Which just leads to another question, how do you do that? By nature, humans seek the path of least resistance. This comes in the form of obtaining a tag, choosing a hunting location, and where you actually hunt at that location. The easiest means in all those scenarios receives the most pressure. So your approach should follow the opposite perspective in all cases. In this chapter we are assuming that you have a high pressured tag, so we skip the obtaining a tag step and focus on how to choose an unpressured hunting location within a pressured unit. There are some simple tried and true methods to avoid pressure. There are also some creative methods that can be employed.

First lets look at the simple tried and true methods. Many tags offer multiple units to hunt in. For example, Colorado OTC tags allow access to literally dozens of hunting units. Some units will be more pressured than others. The hunting statistics posted on each states respective state wildlife website usually lists the amount of hunters that go afield in each unit. This is a great indication of how much pressure is in each unit. Given this data is readily available, a savvy hunter can compare the hunter numbers in the units their tag is good for. Use the description provided in the *research scouting* section of this book to identify units with fewer hunters afield. This is a very simple way to get a head start on avoiding pressure. Many times a hunter will be very surprised to learn just how much pressure certain units have compared to others.

Avoid locations close to cities, towns, recreation areas, and popular trailheads. The more humans that are consistently around, the less game there will be. Hunters will stack up in popular and easy to access public land areas. This is because of ease of access and also because many hunters simply do not do any research and don't know anywhere else to go. If it is easy to find on a map and close to town, there will likely be a lot of pressure. In addition to hunters, you may find yourself competing with hikers, dog walkers, sightseers, cross country skiers, and fishermen. Do a bit of map reading and locate out of the way areas.

The next method comes as no surprise. Head back, way back, into the National Forest and stay away from the access points and maintained trails. This method is certainly tried and true and is the most popular method among hunters. Everyone knows that game avoids the public access points and trails, especially in heavy pressure areas. If it is common knowledge that the game will be deep in the woods, why does this method continue to work? The reason is simple. Heading deep into the woods is tiresome, time consuming, and outright difficult sometimes. You increase your chances of getting lost and often have to spend quite a bit of time hiking in the dark. You also must deal with the difficult task of packing out game if you are successful. While these drawbacks are a reality, most only require more effort and planning to overcome. Getting in better shape, waking up earlier, devoting additional time, and improving your backcountry navigation skills solve just about all of these issues. A lot of successful western hunters do not even begin to hunt until they are at least one mile from the trailhead. Savvy hunters will go two to three miles before beginning their hunt. The further you go reduces the hunter pressure. Less pressure equates to better hunting.

Backcountry camping follows the same theme. When your camp is set a distance from the public access point you have already separated yourself from the general hunting public. This method of hunting starts you off deep in the woods, and your hunt usually takes you even further. Backcountry camping is an acquired skill and taste. Many hunters prefer the amenities of modern lodging and technology. For that reason, the backcountry campers enjoy a solitude many hunters rarely enjoy.

The last tried and true method is somewhat less known. Many western hunting areas are far from civilization and from where hunters actually live. That being so, many hunters tend to camp while hunting. As you may have guessed, hunters prefer to hunt directly from their campsites. Areas that have great camping accommodations tend to receive a good bit of pressure. On the contrary, areas that do not allow camping receive considerably less pressure. If you can locate day use only areas or areas that do not allow overnight parking, you can count on their being fewer hunters. Avoid areas with a lot of campsites. If possible, stick to areas that provide for little camping at all. If you must camp in one of these areas, consider driving to a different location to hunt rather than just hunting from camp.

The tried and true methods are well known and usually only require extra effort on the hunters part. However, many creative methods of avoiding hunter pressure exist as well. These methods simply require a little out-of-the-box thinking.

They are based on the assumption that hunters behave in a predictable manner by favoring the path of least resistance. By least resistance I am referring to hunt planning, map reading, driving, hiking, and hunting. Basically all means of reaching a hunting area. Knowing this, think in opposite terms. If hunters gravitate to the obvious and easy to find areas, what areas are overlooked? The best illustration is to give you many examples.

Examples of creative ways to avoid hunter pressure:

Target hunting areas accessed from pull-offs along forest service roads before reaching the main trailhead. Often hunters stack up at the furthest point back in the forest they can drive to and overlook everything prior. Try hunting areas along the forest road.

Target hunting areas accessed from pull-offs along main roads and highways in no proximity to forest service roads. Highways and main roads often border public land and only receive pressure where roads directly penetrate or where trailheads exist. Check to ensure parking is permitted and consider accessing public land from the main road.

Target hunting areas accessed from unmaintained forest roads. The worse the condition the road is in, the fewer hunters will venture down it. Low profile vehicles may not be able to access these roads at all. If the road is in too bad of shape, consider parking at the beginning and walking in.

Target hunting areas accessed from difficult to locate or unmarked public land access roads. One area I continuously hunt is down an unmarked road that crosses private land before turning public. Because the area is somewhat hard to locate it receives less pressure.

Target hunting areas behind geographic obstacles. Most hunters will avoid hunting an area that requires them to paddle across a lake, cross a creek, climb a steep hill, or drop into a deep valley. A spot I sometimes hunt requires a nearly vertical hike for the first three hundred yards after parking. It is a difficult hike, but it is over within fifteen minutes. The terrain on the other side is quite forgiving, and rarely hunted. Likewise, another preferred area I hunt requires a precipitous drop into a ravine and a steep climb up the other side before I start hunting. While initially difficult, I am into good hunting in thirty minutes. Most hunters wouldn't think to venture straight down and then straight up a ravine.

Walk along the border of private ground for some time before heading into the public land. I often will park at a trailhead and tiptoe the edge of the public land for some distance before heading directly into the forest. Most hunters will head straight back from the parking area. Hunting the border of private land also may have spillover benefits.

Use a bicycle to cover long distances. Often public land limits the use of motorized vehicles. However a bicycle will cover long distances much faster than foot travel, especially if the land is somewhat level. One area I hunt has well-maintained forest roads but they are only drivable by forest service employees. By using a bike I quickly travel miles into the woods, and past most of the other hunters on the way. Bicycles can also come in very handy when hauling out game.

Use unique physical features to your benefit. For example, two different areas I hunt have irrigation ditches that I use for backwoods travel. One is to divert spring runoff from a main road and the other is for agricultural purposes. Both rarely have water in them by the time fall rolls around and both serve as great paths through the woods to cover long distances quickly. Interestingly enough, I have yet to see any other hunters use them.

Target areas with extremely difficult terrain. One of my favorite hunting areas is very rugged. Starting from the moment you step out of the truck, there is hardly a piece of flat ground in the area. It is dense forest, very steep, and easy to get lost. It took me a bit of time to learn how to navigate it, but because it is so rough on the hunter, not many people venture into this area. The game doesn't seem to mind though.

Those are just a few intuitive and creative methods to avoid pressure. Countless more exist, and each has a unique characteristic that deters hunters from going afield. If you can find areas that hunters avoid, game tends to remain unaltered. In fact, game sometimes groups up in the unpressured areas. These are referred to as "refuge" areas. If you can locate a refuge area, you can find a lot of game. Similar to refuge areas are escape routes. Geographic features such as saddles and natural bottlenecks may be overcome with spooked game when pressured. Often these are migration routes as well. If you know such an area, you can use hunter pressure to push game to you. You will still need to venture in and scout the area for game presence and/or the needed physical features to be an escape route. In all cases, hunters should bear safety in mind when accessing difficult, distant, or unique terrain. Such geographical characteristics sometimes elevate fatigue or danger levels. Take appropriate precautions and do not get in over your head.

Hunter pressure can be very frustrating and difficult to predict. Each year I come across numerous non-resident hunters who are very disappointed in their hunt. Often the main reason is the amount of pressure they encounter. They see plenty of other hunters, but no game. I have fallen victim to this many times myself; in fact this was one of my motivations in writing this book. Avoiding pressure requires planning. Do not assume that your area will not have many hunters. Hunters tend to focus in on common areas with high-pressure tags. On OTC hunts, I have often found myself patterning hunters just as much as patterning the game. By avoiding hunters, you often find the game. Scouting areas for hunting pressure can be a useful trick. To do so, you simply drive around to specific hunting locations during the actual season to see how many hunters are parked at different locations.

Multiple trucks and campsites indicate high pressure. Finding areas where no vehicles are parked is always a good indicator. Hunting itself includes a lot of trial and error. In this case, error is hunting in areas with a lot of pressure. If your hunting spot has too much pressure, it may be time to look elsewhere. The game certainly will.

If you obtain a high-pressure tag, you will need to consider how you will avoid hunter pressure and locate game. You have many tools in your toolbox. Consider the tried and true methods. Spend some time thinking out of the box. Follow the steps in the *Research Scouting* section and pay specific attention to avoiding pressure. Scour your maps and try to forecast pressure based on the path of least resistance theory. Always have a Plan B and C and don't be afraid to regroup. You may just find a hotspot that other hunters have overlooked.

Chapter 10 – Common Blunders

This reading goes into great detail as to the recommendations for planning and implementing a successful western hunt. What is has yet to do is point out many common mistakes and pitfalls that hunters encounter every year. Common errors can be easily avoided. The easiest way to illustrate them is through a simple listing. I am overly familiar with most of the items listed below because I personally fell victim to them. Hopefully you heed the advice below and do not suffer from the same mistakes.

Examples of common western hunting blunders:

Having too high of expectations. Check the statistics. Most western hunting success rates are low. If you have never hunted out West before, don't expect it to be a walk in the park. Do your research and set your expectations accordingly.

Purchasing high-pressure tags and having trophy expectations. OTC tags, leftover licenses, or any tag that is very easy to obtain typically correlates with lower success rates, many hunters afield, and less than trophy-sized game. Set your expectations accordingly.

Not researching your options before obtaining a tag. There are many states, seasons, and tags offered throughout the West. Many of these hunts are vastly superior to others in terms of success. It is imperative you research your options and make an educated choice on where to apply and hunt.

Not performing any type of scouting. Many hunters show up each year without the slightest clue of game movements or terrain before they arrive. Utilize every resource you have to scout an area before you arrive, whether this is via Internet, phone calls, maps, on foot, or any resources listed in this reading.

Hunting western game like you would hunt eastern whitetails. Western game is nomadic and intolerant of human presence. Avoid hunting close to your vehicle, watching close by fields, or going on short morning and evening hunts. Western game requires western hunting tactics. Research and follow western hunting tactics.

Hunting near human pressure. More pressure equals less game. Avoid trailheads, camping areas, open flat terrain, etc. During hunting season, you usually won't find game close to public access. Take great effort to distance yourself from hunter pressure.

Not being in shape. Western public land hunting is physically demanding. You cannot drive to your tree stand and especially not to a harvested animal. Almost everything requires hiking and carrying large amounts of weight. If you are not in shape, you will not enjoy yourself and will lessen your chances of harvest success.

Getting in over your head with weather, distance, or lack of food and water. Western weather, expanses, and fatigue will turn men into boys very quickly. Be prepared, spend time researching the logistics of your hunt, and plan accordingly. Over pack food and water as this is your fuel.

Hunting with large parties. If you have a lot of hunters in your group, plan on hunting entirely different areas. You cover a lot of ground in western hunting. It is very easy to crowd out one another. More pressure equals less game.

Hunting the wrong elevations. Game uses different elevations for different reasons at different times of the year. Do your scouting research and be sure to be at the right elevation.

Hunting areas based on ease of terrain. Many hunters gravitate to flat and open terrain. Game tends to do the opposite when the hunters arrive. Do not base your plan on attack on easy walking. Elk do not mind steep terrain. Also, do not rely on watching large open meadows during the day. Game will only use these during the very early and late hours, if during the day at all. Pressured elk rarely ever venture into large open meadows during daylight.

Not hunting the early and late hours of the day. We all know game is most active the first and last few hours of the day. However many western hunters don't want to hike in and out of their hunting areas in the dark for fear of getting lost. Don't get in over your head, but you should be focusing your hunting when the game is most active. Hunt the first and last hour in prime locations.

Avoiding draw tags due to inconvenience. Yes, planning years ahead for a potential hunt can be cumbersome and learning the rules and regulations can be confusing. But believe me, you will be very appreciative of your efforts when you complete a successful draw hunt. Even more so, you will surely be kicking yourself when you arrive on OTC hunts to find many hunters and no game. Apply for limited entry tags, even if the drawing doesn't require points.

Hunting later seasons for convenience. Yes, later seasons may have preferred weapon types and season dates, but these are the last hunters in line each year. Many bulls have been harvested, severely pressured, or have broken antlers. Try to hunt the earlier seasons when the game is less pressured, even if this requires you use a different weapon type or enter a harder draw.

Being a fair weather hunter. Western game often inhabits hard to reach places. Winter weather often pushes game down in elevation and much closer to public access points. Do not throw in the towel when the weather turns sour. Sometimes this can be the best time to be in the field.

Not having the right gear. Western hunting can be very demanding on the hunter. Quality boots, packs, clothing, and gear can be the difference between early fatigue and harvest success. Be sure to acquire necessary and quality gear before heading out.

Hunting pressured areas and not relocating. Too much pressure will cause game to leave an area. The game likely will not return during your hunt. Have a plan B and C hunting area and do not be afraid to utilize them.

Some of the items discussed here are overall themes of this book. Other items are much more subtle. When chasing game, try to think like game. They will do everything they need to satisfy their needs and to avoid you. Go the extra mile when planning and executing your hunt. It will separate you from the bulk of the hunters. Avoid the common blunders.

Bull Elk Harvested During Blizzard, Colorado

Chapter 11 - Logistics Planning

Closely related to hunt planning is arranging the logistics of your trip. Logistics planning comes in many forms, but the most significant are lodging, transportation, and sustenance (i.e., food & water). These three themes are dependant upon one another given the choices you make. We will touch briefly upon each subject. After touching on the three main forms of logistics planning we will briefly touch on recommended gear.

Deciding on your lodging is the initial logistics decision, as most other decisions will differ depending on your lodging choice. Lodging comes in four main types. In order of increasing hunter effort, these forms are hotel/cabin rental, trailer campers, car camping, and backcountry camping. The decision to book a hotel is usually based on comfort preference rather than hunting technique. In doing so, you have the advantage of a comfortable bed, a hot shower, a broad choice of meals, shelter from the elements, and all the amenities of a normal dwelling. Many hunting seasons occur when temperatures turn cold and many hunters wish to avoid sleeping in freezing temperatures. It also may offer a better opportunity to dry clothing and organize gear. One can certainly argue the benefits of this choice. It keeps the hunter well rested and nourished during the hunt. However, there are many drawbacks. The first to mention is transportation related. This method of lodging is rarely next to your hunting location. That means you will need to provide more time for driving, loading and unloading gear, and time spent on the trail on your way to your hunting area. It keeps you furthest from game and requires you put in significant effort to reach prime hunting areas each day. Given the time lost from transportation, you often find yourself going to bed later and waking up earlier. It can also be pricey to book lodging. In fact, it is usually the most expensive of all methods. I recommend using this choice if you highly value personal comfort, have the possibility of harsh weather, or lack the knowledge and resources for camping. A quick Internet search for hotels, motels, or cabins in the closest towns to your hunting area should reveal your lodging options with this choice. Ensure the lodging has all the amenities you require and remember the closer it is to your hunting area the better off you are.

Trailer camping is a hybrid technique that brings your lodging to your camping area. It has many of the benefits of a motel and usually eliminates a good bit of the transportation issue. This method will provide a comfortable bed and possibly a stove, microwave, and warm shower depending on the amenities of your camper. It also keeps you sheltered from the elements, but to a lesser degree than a hotel. Keep in mind that many public land areas have specific usage rules and may not allow camping. Many public land roads are not in very good shape or do not have suitable flat land to park a trailer. In such cases you may need to park your trailer somewhere other than where you will be hunting. You will also need to hike into your hunting area and will spend significant time travelling on foot, albeit much less than if you were in a motel in a nearby town. Getting your camper to your hunting area may be costly as well. It will require a heavy-duty vehicle to pull the camper and tends to be a bit tougher on gas mileage. Some hunters pull them across the country and others rent them from nearby towns. Be sure to complete a cost comparison with the other lodging options as trailer rental and transportation costs can get very high. You should also ensure you are comfortable with the amenities of your camper. Once again, a quick Internet search should reveal the camper options of both renting from your hometown or in a town near where you will be hunting. Amenities should be listed online as well. Consider your hunting needs, preferences, budget, and the logistics of this method before renting a camper.

The next method to discuss is car camping. This term simply refers to some form of camping very close to your vehicle. It usually involves a tent or some kind of temporary shelter that you assemble alongside your parking area and a maintained road. Many tents ranging in size and quality exist on the market today. A favorite for western hunters is the large canvas wall tent that incorporates a wood stove as a heat source, but you will see all makes and manners of tents and shelters across the West during hunting seasons each year. This method is one step down in terms of comfort from a trailer. Then again, you often can place tents in many areas where trailers cannot go. They are significantly cheaper and take up much less space. You also do not have to ponder transportation and rental logistics. In addition, you have your vehicle close by if you need to travel to a different hunting area, go to town for supplies, or simply store the majority of your gear. But what you gain in ease of use you lose in terms of amenities. You now must deal with the elements, accommodate a usable bed, forego showers, and put more effort into cooking and storing food. Outfitting a camping hunt is somewhat of an art as each hunter usually has a preferred method to provide the essentials for their trip. You will need shelter, warmth, food, water, and a dry place to securely store your gear. The best education for setting up such a hunt is experience. Those who camp often may find this method second nature and are very familiar with the living style and necessities. If you have little experience, take a camping trip or two before embarking on your trip to ensure you have your method and essentials accounted for. Many websites, books, and online forums discuss how to accommodate the needs of a campsite. Use rational planning and be sure to think through the incorporation of your hunting needs. Before starting off ensure you may camp in your intended hunting location.

The last type of accommodation is by far the best method for western hunting. Backcountry camping eliminates nearly all of the transportation needed while hunting. It is the method of camping wherein a hunter packs their camp into the woods and sets up camp at a distance from their vehicle and much closer to where they will be hunting. It places you very far from roads, trailheads, and human activity in general. This is where the game lives. Putting yourself one step closer gives you a leg up in timing, travel, transportation, and also insight to game habits. It separates you from other hunters and usually allows you to travel further into the backcountry. It provides a great experience and definitely has the greatest benefits for the actual hunt. On the flip side, this method requires a hunter to forego all the amenities associated with the other forms of accommodations.

You will need to bring everything you need with you into the backcountry. You will also need to bring everything out, including game if you are successful. This is what deters most hunters from this method. Outfitters use horses and mules. Some DIY hunters do as well. Horses enable you to carry considerably more gear, but they also need to be owned or rented, cared for, and transported to your hunting area. This can be quite an undertaking and if you wish to learn to care for horses you will need to gain that knowledge firsthand. Many DIY hunters prefer to backpack. Carrying all of your gear on your back requires it to be very lightweight. This is much more of an art than car camping and the needed gear can also be costly.

Experience is the only good teacher here. I recommend all hunters who wish to backcountry camp embark on a practice trip before their actual hunt. You will quickly learn how essential it is to have lightweight gear. This requires you to accommodate only the bare necessities. The good news is that many simple methods now exist to filter and sanitize water, which means you may not have to lug all your water in on your back. Head to a quality camping store and discuss your situation. You will need shelter, warmth, food, water, and a dry place to securely store your gear. You also need to do this comfortably enough to actually hunt and enjoy your trip. When backcountry camping, be sure you do not place your camp where you specifically intend to hunt. Game quickly learns of your presence and moves out when you move in. Ideally you should set camp at least a half mile downwind from where you plan to hunt. But you will need to reason based on your specific situation. Backcountry camping is an art, and loved by those who continuously do it. Give it a try, you just may get hooked.

Hiking in a Backcountry Camp, Colorado

With all types of camping, safety is a high concern. Be sure to carry a safety kit when hunting and camping. Experience will hone your skills and give you an idea of the needed gear. Be sure your camping location is out of harms way. That means avoiding dead trees and branches, rain runoff and flood areas, wind swept areas, irresponsible fires, and hungry wildlife. Bear country has specific concerns with food treatment and what to do if an encounter occurs. Maintain all cooking, eating, cleaning, and food storage at least one hundred feet downwind from your sleeping area. Always let someone know where you are. If you are a novice, don't get in over your head. Backcountry camping takes practice, do not risk getting lost, over straining yourself, depriving yourself of sustenance, or spoiling harvested game.

Planning for transportation is somewhat simple. You will need to travel from your home to your hunting accommodations. This involves either flying or driving. Many hunters choose to fly because it is much faster. Flying then requires you obtain a vehicle to travel from the airport to the hunting unit. You will also need a vehicle from your accommodations to your hunting area. If you plan to hunt anytime after mid-September, snow is possible. If you plan to hunt anytime after mid-October, snow is probable. Your vehicle will need four-wheel drive to navigate public land roads just about any time of year. Throw some weather into the mix and you will need a high profile vehicle with four-wheel drive. Most 4x4 trucks will do the job pretty easily. Trucks also offer a bed for carrying gear and downed game. Flying saves time and keeps you from driving long distances across the country, but it limits the amount of gear you can bring. This can be a major issue. Taking firearms on domestic flights is quite easy, simply contact your local airport and inquire as to the procedures. It is extremely difficult to fly with all the gear needed for camping. But it is not so difficult if you plan to hunt out of a motel. Flying with harvested meat is also an issue. Most domestic flights allow frozen meat in coolers as checked bags. But this can get costly as a harvested elk may fill multiple coolers. You may consider shipping or donating the meat, but ensure your plans before counting on this method. When it comes to shipping meat, there is no cheap way about it. First you will need to purchase and assemble acceptable packaging and then you will need to pay a shipping company to send it to your home. With the weight of meat, this gets very pricey. Some butcher shops offer shipping, but do not expect this to be any cheaper. Call ahead and research different methods for shipping game.

Once again, simple online searches procure plane tickets and rental vehicles. UPS, FedEx, and the US postal Service are the three main companies that will offer meat-shipping options. A quick call or Internet search will reveal the prices and options available. Overall, you will need to consider your specific situation and whether you think flying and renting a vehicle is more feasible then just driving across the country.

Due to gear, vehicle, and shipping concerns, most hunters choose to drive out West for hunts. It may take a bit longer, but you will not have to deal with any of the issues explained in the previous paragraph. Simply load up the truck and make the long drive to your hunting accommodations.

When done, you load up the truck and drive back. If hunters travel together, they can rotate driving to stay on the road longer for better time. Driving takes a good bit longer from point A to point B, but it is much simpler. Complete a cost comparison and weigh the pros and cons of both choices.

Sustenance can be difficult to plan for. Try to think of it in simple terms at first and then break into the minute details. You will need food and water for the duration of your trip. You should plan on needing about a gallon of water each day. This is easy to access in a motel. When camping, most hunters bring large multi-gallon water containers and refill when needed. If you are backcountry camping, you will need to bring water with you or locate a source and purify it when you arrive. This is not as hard as it sounds and just about every outdoor store these days sells water purification and filtering kits. Western hunting is very active, so count on at least three hearty meals a day and a way to cook and store them. This is simple in a motel, not so much when camping, and even harder when backcountry camping. The timing of and actual food in your meals is up to you, but your cooking and storage methods will strongly influence it. Most hunters eat a quick bite before hunting in the morning, pack a high calorie lunch while on the hunt, and eat dinner after the hunt. On all day hunts, I actually pack two lunches, one for late morning and one for early afternoon. Given the high amount of physical activity in western hunting, four small meals throughout the day works well. Meals should be high in calories, protein, and carbohydrates to enable improved physical activity. Lunches should be as lightweight as possible. If you are in a motel or cabin, you may have access to a stove, microwave, and refrigerator. Thus your meal preparation is quite simple. If you are using a camper or car camping, you likely will have a stove or fire of some sort and coolers to store food. Plan accordingly. If backcountry camping, you will need to carry extremely lightweight meals in with you and have a means of cooking them. Most carry multiple food items that do not require cooking and supplement this diet with freeze-dried meals that only require boiling water to prepare. This still requires a method of heating water, but many small stoves are available on the market today. Take time to plan your food and water resources on a hunting trip. This is the fuel that will keep you going during your hunt. As with camping, most hunters quickly develop their own tried and true techniques in meal preparation.

A weeklong car camping hunt for me typically includes:

Daily breakfast: bagel with peanut butter or two oatmeal packets.
Daily lunches: two Cliff Bars, two sandwiches, two boiled eggs, apple, pretzels.
Daily dinners: A freeze-dried meal with wraps or a one-course meal (such as precooked rice, meat, and vegetables frozen in Tupperware beforehand) with wraps.

There are countless options and methods for food preparation and you will quickly develop your own. Keep in mind your meals should be easily prepared, easily cleaned up after, and high in protein. For this reason, freeze dried meals such as *Mountain House* and *Backpackers Pantry* have become very popular in recent years.

Make sure you place significant emphasis on sustenance when planning for your western hunting trip. Consider your personal preferences when making decisions. Utilize Internet searches to weigh different options. If you plan to camp, gain experience camping before you set foot in the field. It can become a matter of survival if you did not plan properly. Remember, you're out hunting to have a pleasurable experience as well as harvest game. Be sure you are happy and comfortable with the logistics decisions you make.

Chapter 12 - Gear

The appropriate gear to bring hunting is always a hot topic among hunters. As with all sports, there are hunters who must have the most cutting edge products available. Other hunters get by with the rustic gear that they were handed down years ago. Many of us fall somewhere in between. So which group has the right idea? The answer is everyone, as long as their gear meets their personal needs.

Rather than focusing on brands or technologies, a hunter should focus on utility. Ask yourself what purpose needs served, and then what is the best way to serve that purpose. Ask two hunters about their preferences and you will get two different answers. In this reading, we will focus on the purpose served and then you can decide on the best brand and technique based on your personal preferences. Given the variations in travel and lodging, we will just focus on what you need for a full day of hunting. The reader can then make determinations and variations from there.

The initial item to consider is clothing. First and foremost, weather comes to mind. Typical western hunting encompasses full days of hunting, from before dawn until after dusk. It also includes hiking for a large portion of that time. You will need to research the weather of your hunt. One can easily do so with brief Internet searches on weather websites for the closest town to your hunting area. Look up the time of year you will be hunting, the average temperatures, and the average precipitation. Take into account you may be at a higher elevation than the closest town, which means the weather will be slightly colder. Across the Rockies, you should be prepared for both rain and snow during your hunt. This includes wind and subfreezing temperatures. In my experience, the most important piece of gear you can have is your boots. You will be putting miles on them and they cover the first body part to fatigue. A good metaphor is that of a vehicle. You would not take a small economy car off-roading. You would want a strong engine with high clearance that you can count on. Likewise, your boots need to be ready to carry you for miles in broken terrain. They need to be quality, waterproof, broken-in, and designed for mountain hiking. If there is one item I recommend spending a few more dollars on, it is boots. Just because your current boots work for short distances or tree-stand hunting doesn't mean they will carry you miles through rocky canyons, streams, snow, and steep hillsides. They may not fall apart, but boots not meant for aggressive mountain hiking cause foot fatigue. Choose a proven name and be sure to spend many hours breaking them in before trekking miles into the backwoods. While breaking them in, attempt to cover terrain similar to what you will be hunting on (i.e. off trail steep terrain). This should give you a good idea as to if they will be sufficient for western hunting. If your feet still quickly fatigue after they are broken in, you may need to choose a different pair. In addition, pay close attention to your choice of socks. Many brands exist today that are specifically meant for hiking or hunting. Wool seems to be the best footwear in terms of warmth. Ensure you have ample pairs to keep your feet dry during your hunt.

Choosing clothing is similar to planning for other hunting trips. The main difference is that you are doing a bit more hiking rather than just sitting while hunting. Choose comfortable lightweight materials. Layering is the best technique for ensuring needed warming and cooling. Try to choose quiet clothing as well. Make sure your wardrobe matches the temperature range and precipitation of your hunt, and that you have sufficient changes of clothes if you get wet. Waterproof materials are always a bonus. Think in terms of lightweight, durable, and quiet. Many brands offer many different options that will suit your specific needs. You simply need to research the weather and terrain you will be hunting and match your clothing accordingly. In wet conditions, you will also need a means of drying boots and clothing before using them again.

In terms of weapons, beauty is in the eye of the beholder. Each state issues minimum weapon/firearm requirements to pursue each type of game. For bows this usually consists of bow type, broadhead requirements, and draw weight. For rifles this usually consists of minimum calibers, foot-pounds of energy, barrel lengths, and bullet weight. You will need to look to the state specific regulations to see what is the minimum requirement of each state. While many feel that bigger is always better, most experts maintain that each hunter should utilize the weapon that suits them best, save to say that it is within legal requirements. In short, most deer hunting bows, rifles, and muzzleloaders are more than sufficient for western game as well. The best weapon and caliber all depends on the preference of who is using the weapon. The more popular rifles are the .270, 7mm magnum, .30'6, and 300 magnum, in no specific order. All of these calibers are more than sufficient. Given the amount of hiking involved in western hunting, ensure you equip any rifle with a quality shoulder strap. Follow the state requirements and use the weapon you are most comfortable with. The same concept holds true with ammunition. Choose the correct tool for the job. Ensure you have the appropriate caliber and quality for the game you are hunting. Large animals are hard to take down and higher quality ammunition is worth its weight in gold when big game hunting. The minimum recommended bullet weight for elk is 150 grains. Find ammunition that works well with your firearm and that you are comfortable with.

Optics seems to be more of a question than weapon caliber in western hunting. The proper optics depends on the type of terrain you will be hunting. Given the research performed when planning a hunt, you should know if you are hunting in open terrain, rolling hills, or dense forest. Open areas are a bit more demanding when considering your optics. In open areas, I always carry a long-range scope (such as a 4x12x40), a range finder, and quality binoculars. For instance, most antelope hunting is done in wide-open terrain. That being so, many shots are done at distances out to three or four hundred yards. Long distance shooting requires greater magnification on a riflescope. It is also imperative to know precise target distances to account for bullet trajectory. That means you need a rangefinder. Most boxes of quality ammunition include a ballistics table on the back that states the precise drop of the ammunition at different distances. Range your target, know your bullet drop, wind speed, and practice accordingly. Likewise, binoculars are heavily used for glassing open terrain. They are much easier to use than bringing up your riflescope every time you wish to look at something. For all long range shooting, ensure you practice and have the capability to make shots at long distances. Only attempt shots you are comfortable with. If you plan to glass extremely long distances (over a mile), you will need a spotting scope. Once again, many brands exist boasting different levels of quality for all optics. It is up to the hunter to research specific models, prices, and needs regarding an upcoming hunt. Long distance game judgment and shooting takes practice. Remember that there are many types of big game out West; many hunters end up with hefty fines each year for improperly harvesting incorrect game animals (e.g. mistaking a moose for an elk). Ensure you are practiced, capable, and comfortable before pulling the trigger on a long shot. If hunting dense vegetation or timbered forests where the visibility is limited, you may be able to leave the rangefinder and binoculars at home. Much of the elk hunting in forested mountain ranges will not require long shooting as you may only be able to see 100-200 yards. Thus the common 3x9x40 scope is more than sufficient. If you have any chance of precipitation on your hunt, ensure you bring a scope cover. Many hunters each year fog their scopes with snow and rain and are incapable of shooting when they finally see game. Plastic flip scope covers are cheap and easy to use. You can find these at most sporting goods stores.

In terms of required gear quality, next in line to your boots is your pack. You will be hunting long days in the backcountry and will need to carry quite a bit of supplies. The best method to do so is by using a daypack. The most common form is an internal frame backpack. Any number of models can be purchased. Your pack will carry food, water, excess clothing, and various pieces of gear. While hunters should attempt to go a lightweight as possible, your pack should be able to accommodate the space and weight of an elk quarter if need be. To distribute weight properly, I recommend an internal frame (rather than external) pack with chest and waist straps. Water bladders are also much more convenient than water bottles. Heavier items in your pack should be placed high near your shoulders and close to your back. Research a few pack options based on the amount of gear you intend to bring. Put some time and effort into choosing a quality backpack and try it on before purchasing it. Your body will thank you for having a quality pack.

So what should go into your daypack? The necessary optics and clothing have already been discussed. These items can be stored in you pack when not being used, but the primary purpose of your pack should be to carry food and water. When active, we consume about a gallon of water per day. Much of that will be consumed before and after you hunt and you will need to make a personal judgment call as to how much to bring with you when hunting. Typical backpack water bladders hold around 64 ounces of liquid (half gallon). On very hot days, this seems to be about what I require for a full day hunt. On cold days, I usually only need about half that much. Become familiar with your personal needs and practice in the off-season. Consider the amount of time you plan to be in the field and plan accordingly. You should also budget for needed water if you are successful and have to pack out game. Food is handled in a similar manner, plan in terms of your personal needs. The standard caloric intake is a diet of 2,000 calories per day. You will need significantly more than this when putting in a full day of weathered hiking. As previously mentioned, I carry two lunches during a full day of hunting. This is in addition to breakfast before setting out and dinner after returning. My lunches consist of high calorie and protein foods. You should focus on nutritious foods that give you energy and reduce fatigue. Avoid junk food if possible. I will be the first to admit that I am not the healthiest hunter in the woods, but I take extra effort when packing my lunches so I have more energy. Research foods with a high value to weight ratio that are easily prepared and have little to no waste product. I have a developed a standard lunch over the years that is based on my personal preference that I shared in the previous chapter. Yours will differ, but just ensure it meets your demands and tailor it accordingly as you gain experience. The items discussed in the next few paragraphs will be part of your daypack as well.

Next you should think to navigation. In terms of navigation, many hunters carry a map, compass, and global positioning system (GPS), all of which they constantly use when hunting. Hard copy maps are great for planning. I constantly pour over these before, during, and after hunts to plan. You can view much more ground at one time with a hard copy map than on a handheld GPS. A compass is a great tool for orientation while hunting. I constantly take bearings and use them to help guide me from point A to point B and to note wind direction. While they are certainly not as advanced as a GPS, they are much faster, simpler, and do not run out of batteries. For years I did not own or use a GPS. I simply used a map and compass. Upon purchasing one, I can never go back. They make you a much more efficient hunter. A GPS comes in very handy when navigating new terrain and moving in the dark. Dependency on these tends to lessen as you become more familiar with an area, but they are great at pinpointing and saving exact locations. I constantly mark waypoints at wallows, glassing points, saddles, and anywhere I want to come back to. You can then come directly back to waypoints from any direction. A GPS is priceless when scouting or hunting new terrain. You never have to second guess going deeper into the woods or getting lost. Just be sure to carry extra batteries. In addition, they are a great method of finding an exact location, such as your truck, in the dark. For safety sake, I keep all three on me in the field. The compass and map come cheap. I like to purchase waterproof maps that depict public land boundaries, access roads, and elevation topography. The map should also be at a usable scale. I prefer the scale to be at 1:50,000 or larger. GPS devices range quite a bit more in price and quality. Some are basic while other have just about every bell and whistle you can think of. You can even obtain GPS applications on smart phones. Find one that meets your needs and budget.

At a minimum they should show topography and geographical features. Ones that show public land boundaries come in very handy. I certainly recommend them for every western hunter, especially if hunting in an unfamiliar area. In addition to these items and for general safety, you should always let someone know where you plan on hunting and when you plan to return. Have a check in plan with a friend or relative so that if you do run into trouble someone will quickly notice.

A safety kit is a must whenever you are in the backcountry. Miles from the trailhead or your vehicle, you can find yourself in quite the predicament if you do not have basic medical supplies. Most outdoor stores offer full medical kits that are very compact. You can find many different recommendations of what should be included in such medical kits. If you are unsure of what to carry, look at the contents a few medical kits at your local outdoor store to see what is included. Complete an Internet search on what is recommended by backcountry professionals. Personally, I build my medical kits rather than purchase them over the counter. While my kit may not be the best method for you, I will share what mine includes all the same. My medical kit includes: a small roll of medical tape, an emergency blanket, super glue, a few band aids, Neosporin, Ibuprofen, waterproof matches, a lighter, a magnesium fire starter tool, and a whistle.

At some point in your hunt you will likely be hiking in the dark. Maybe you will be following a blood trail or trying to find a specific hunting blind. All nigh time travel requires some type of artificial light. Flashlight technology these days is impressive, especially when you consider light emitting diode (LED) lights. Very small LED flashlights are very powerful. I carry both a small headlamp and a small flashlight while hunting. Both are very lightweight and take up little room. The headlamp is useful for hands free lighting when hiking and completing tasks. The flashlight is useful when you need a little bit more power for locating things at a distance. It also gives you piece of mind to have a back up light if one fails. Use your best judgment when choosing what lighting to bring while hunting. Keep in mind that having lightweight equipment is essential on western hunts.

A quality knife should be part of every hunter's repertoire. You will need this knife for miscellaneous tasks, but mostly for breaking down harvested game. I prefer bigger knives, but any knife that is at least four inches and sharp is practical enough to gut and quarter western game. Hunters will have their own preference. Choose knives with a quality blade. The key is ensuring your knife is sharp. The last thing you want is to fatigue yourself forcing a dull blade through an elk cape and quarters. I also carry a bone saw when western hunting. Many types exist, but I prefer a standard eighteen-inch hacksaw with replaceable blades. This easily fits into a daypack and can be purchased at most hardware stores.

Downed western game is too big to drag. With the distances you will hike, packing out meat usually requires quartering or deboning in the field. A quality knife and saw is needed for this. As the focus of this reading is on hunt planning, we will not spend much time on how to properly quarter or debone game. Before embarking on a western hunt you should complete basic research enough to be able to complete these tasks in the field. Having someone walk you through it the first time is very helpful. The best teacher is experience. If you have no one to teach you, you can find videos online or read detailed accounts in hunting books. YouTube is a great source for this. Elk are much larger than whitetails and quartering difficulty is multiplied by their sheer size. Forget about dragging them any distance, and be sure not to strain or fatigue yourself, as you will likely be at a good distance from your vehicle. Some hunters hang and skin their game in the field, others wait until the quarters are back at camp before skinning. All efforts in processing downed game should be to preserve the meat. This means ensuring it gets cooled as quickly as possible. At a minimum, you need to remove the back straps, tenderloins, four quarters, and antlers from your downed animal. If you plan to have it mounted, you will need to cape and remove the head. Below is a brief overview of the process.

With an elk lying in front of you, the first thing to do is gut it. This requires the hunter to cut the skin from the genitals to the sternum and remove all organs in the stomach and chest cavity. This helps cool the game. You should also drag the guts a distance away from the animal. This attracts scavenging animals to the gut pile and not to the carcass. With the guts removed, you can then quickly remove the tenderloins. These are two small steaks on the inside of the stomach cavity near the backbone and situated near the hindquarters. These elongated steaks are removed by pulling on them with one hand and cutting the connective tissue with your knife in your other hand. Next, roll the animal on its side and proceed to remove the first front quarter by pushing the leg away from the body and cutting up the natural seam under the front leg pit. Basically, cut up through the armpit while placing outward tension on the front leg. The front shoulder comes off surprisingly easy without having to cut any bone. Similarly, cut up the back leg pit and remove the hindquarter. Push the hind leg away from the body and slice through the connective tissue in the genital region continuously moving toward the backbone. As you cut further you will encounter the ball joint that connects the leg to the hipbone. You can either cut around the ball joint or saw through it on their underside. Continue putting pressure on the leg away from the body and slice deeper through the flesh until the leg is completely removed. You often need to carefully cut the remaining flesh from back angle to remove the entire hindquarter. You can then roll the animal over and repeat this for the quarters on the other side. Next, begin on the back straps. Ensure the skin and fur from the area on either side of the backbone from the neck down to the tail is completely removed. Tightly along the backbone, insert your knife and deeply slice from the where the neck meets the shoulders all the way down to the tail. Do this on either side of the backbone and stay as close to the backbone as possible. You will then make a forty-five degree angle cut from where the back strap meets the ribcage toward the backbone. Slice from the same insertion point at the neck to the to the same ending point at the tail. The back straps are

145

somewhat triangular in shape, thus the point of your knife meets the initial backbone cut to separate the meat from the animal. In this manner, remove both back straps. Afterwards, use your saw to remove the antlers, skull, or head depending on what you wish to do with your trophy. You can also use your saw to sever the legs at the knees and elbows to reduce carry weight. Once again, these actions are much better shown than explained. Utilize online videos or have someone assist you your first time.

Using a Tree Branch to Pack out Elk Quarters, Colorado

Game quartering bags are a great tool to protect meat when hauling it out of the woods. I don't usually keep these on me while hunting. I will carry the first load back to the vehicle un-skinned to protect the meat from damage. I then skin it at my vehicle, put it in the cloth quartering bag, and place it in the shade. I then head back in for another load. Anything I left in the field was promptly skinned and hung in the shade when I quartered it. I then use quartering bags while hauling it out of the woods. Elk quarters can weigh 30-80 pounds. In addition, you have back straps, tenderloins, and the antlers to carry. It is your call as to how much weight you carry on each trip. Often I will fashion a tree branch with a front quarter hanging from each side for my first trip out of the woods. I place it evenly across my shoulders and hike out. I also leave an aluminum external frame backpack in my truck when hunting. I use this to carry out the remaining pieces on subsequent pack trips. Count on a full size elk taking two to four trips to pack out. It just depends how ambitious you are and how far back the animal is. Hunters also employ sleds, bicycles, and horses to assist in this process. Many hunters prefer to debone game. This method takes more time but eliminates a good deal of carrying weight. It essentially follows the same procedure as described above, but goes further to remove all meat from the quarters. You can put the deboned meat in a pack and carry it out. Whatever method you choose to employ, ensure you are well versed in the technique before beginning. Take care to cool your meat as soon as possible. The best way to do so is to hang it in a shady tree while processing and hauling out your game. For this, you will need to carry rope in your backpack. Parachute cord is durable, lightweight, and takes up very little room. I carry at least 30 feet in my backpack when hunting.

The last item to consider is calls and attractants. If you plan to hunt during the rut, having a call or two mastered is a good idea. While bugles can be useful, cow calls are more popular in usage. Research a few brands and capabilities. Learn to use the calls through video and audio presentations. If hunting during the rut, it is a good idea to have a bugle and cow call on you at all times. It is also very helpful to have a push button cow call handy when hiking. If you accidently scare elk, a quick mew on this call may briefly delay the game from spooking. Rattling for elk is also effective and gaining popularity, but antlers can be a cumbersome item to carry on an elk hunt. Likewise, scents and attractants are growing in popularity. I always carry elk cover scent to mask my human odor. This is in addition to taking scent eliminating showers and using scent control clothing.

At the end of the day, your pack should include the tools required for the hunt and personal preference items. I gave you my perspective on what a pack should include. It is up to you to decide what you carry for the day.

In summary, my gear recommendation for each full day in western hunting is:

Appropriate clothing for layering
Quality boots
Weapon with ammunition
Backpack containing:
 64oz water bladder
 Two lunches
 Binoculars & rangefinder (if hunting open terrain)
 Map
 Compass
 GPS with extra batteries
 Safety kit
 Knife
 Saw
 Headlight
 Flashlight
 30' parachute cord
 Game calls
 Cell phone
 Camera
 Toilet paper

  The logistics and gear sections of this book are brief and very general in nature. They simply provide notification to hunters that these are the items they should be specifically planning for. It is up to the hunter to make decisions, use logic to plan, and research details further if they still have question. Quick Internet searches will reveal many options. Gear comes in many shapes and forms and really boils down to necessity and hunter preference. Search for competitive prices and weigh your options. Focus on lightweight materials. Try out your gear before taking it hunting. It doesn't have to be hunting season to enjoy the outdoors!

Chapter 12 - Physical Conditioning

As the majority of this reading pertains to planning your hunt in the off-season, an emphasis on physical fitness is due. Hopefully my earlier descriptions of the Rocky Mountains painted a picture of the terrain for you. Somewhere in that picture should be the sheer elevation gain typical to the majority of the region. The Rockies are steep and unforgiving. To hunt in them, you need to traverse this terrain as the game does.

The animals in the Rockies change with the terrain. Goats and sheep inhabit the upper reaches that seem almost impossible to navigate. As you descend, the landscape becomes somewhat more forgiving, but it is still very difficult. Elk, moose, and deer exist to varying degrees and travel from above tree line in the summer down to the low valleys in the winter. As a common rule of thumb, the higher you are in elevation, the more steep and demanding the land is. Public land was also set-aside after many generations of pioneers and land claims. That means most of the easily accessible ground is private land. As less forgiving land usually keeps out humans, animals often gravitate to the inhospitable areas or regions far from vehicle access. Expect to travel to these areas on foot, and often without trails. You should have researched the terrain in the area you are hunting long before you arrive. Given the type of game, season, weather, and access, you should have somewhat of an idea what you are getting yourself into. Rest assured you will probably end up hiking further than you had originally planned.

These explanations point to one simple concept: to hunt in the Rocky Mountains you need to be in good physical shape. The hunting methods employed in western hunting require long-winded hikes up and down steep terrain. You probably will not be sitting in tree stands or hunting even remotely close to your vehicle. Enduring long hikes at high elevations requires that you prepare two parts of your body. These are your lungs and your muscles.

Fatigued First Time Western Hunter, Colorado

Many individuals new to the West do not realize the effect higher elevations have on your breathing habits. Higher elevations have less oxygen. The higher you go the less of it there is. Research what elevation you will be hunting at. Many US citizens live close to sea level. For perspective, the mountains in Colorado range roughly from 5,000 to 14,000 feet. You can count on hunting somewhere in between. The message here is not very complicated. Exercise your lungs through extensive cardiovascular activity. Cardiovascular exercises take many forms; you simply need to give your lungs a workout on a consistent basis before you arrive. Some examples are playing sports, jogging, bicycling, hiking, etc. This should strengthen your lungs and make you more amiable to high elevation breathing. Going from low to high elevations affects individuals in different ways, inevitably some much more than others. If you are a smoker, the effects may be compounded. It takes time to acclimate to higher climates. Some hunters spend a day in middle elevations to ready themselves before they ascend higher, but many do not have the time or means to do so. Simply understand that your body will react differently to lower oxygen levels and you will find it harder to breath during physical activity. Strengthening your lungs prior to the season will aid your breathing during your hunt. Even so, you inevitably will find yourself breathing a bit harder than you would if you were at lower elevations.

You should also be aware of the symptoms and effects of altitude sickness. Altitude sickness affects individuals when they fail to obtain enough oxygen at high altitudes. Most of the symptoms are minor and include headache, loss of appetite, fatigue, and difficulty sleeping. But more severe symptoms of faintness, confusion, discoloration, and ataxia do occur sometimes. Altitude sickness is most associated with individuals who are not acclimated to high elevations that ascend quickly from low to high elevations. High elevations are commonly referred to as 8,000 feet or higher.[vi] Mild altitude sickness is common. According to studies at the High Altitude Research Center at the University of Colorado, more than 20% of people visiting high elevations get altitude sickness in the United States. Aside from the elevation of where you call home, there really isn't any rhyme or reason as to who is affected and who is not. Often you just need time for your body to acclimate. Be sure to keep yourself hydrated and take headache medicine if need be. The only true cure for altitude sickness is descending to lower elevations. Be mindful of the symptoms and prepared to descend to lower elevations if they become significant.

Now that we have touched on keeping your lungs in shape, let's discuss keeping your muscles on par as well. Consider a typical day of western hunting. You will likely rise in the early hours of the morning and hit the trail long before daylight. Your goal will be to reach a vantage point for glassing, a wooded area for stalking, or an interception point for calling or tracking. These areas will likely be miles from your vehicle or camping area. Whether you hunt just the morning or a full day, you will likely be on your feet for the majority of your hunt. You will traverse trails, off-trail terrain, blow down areas, up hills, down hills, and through rocky areas. You may encounter snow, ice, rain, thunderstorms, bitter cold, and even heat. Horses may make your life easier, but even if you have horses you will still be doing the majority of your actual hunting on foot. Throughout all this travel you will also be carrying a weapon and a pack. In addition, you need to be mentally focused on the hunt and prepared for a steady shot at any time. When all is said and done you want to be physically ready to wake up and do it all over again, often for multiple days. To top it all off, if you are lucky enough to harvest an animal, that is when the work really begins. Quartering and hanging an animal can be tough on your own, and an elk quarter can weigh thirty to eighty pounds. That's a lot of weight on your shoulders and a lot of trips in rough terrain.

Western hunting is physically demanding. Consistent cardiovascular exercise is extremely helpful in preparation. Weight training is a good idea as well. Your leg muscles need strengthening for the long hikes, and your arms, shoulders, and back need strengthening for carrying your weapon, pack, and harvested game. These are rather simple concepts. But what is often overlooked is how the terrain you will be traversing affects your body. Hiking long distances, off-trail, while carrying heavy gear, has an effect on your body that cannot be replicated by the treadmill or bench press. The terrain you will be walking on is uneven, rough, and often at strange and inconsistent angles, such as walking along steep hillsides. This strains your feet especially, but your ankles, knees, and back as well. The best way to ready yourself is to replicate this type of activity as much as you can. Go on long off trail hikes over rough terrain with a heavy pack. Even if you do not live near mountains, seek out difficult hiking areas where you can. This could mean repetitiously hiking small hills or river drainages. Consistently repeat hiking exercises before the hunting seasons. Scouting the hunting area in the off-season serves a dual purpose and is a great way to exercise. Many non-residents will not have this option but can still get out in local parks and forests for hiking exercise. If you are unable to replicate long and strenuous hikes, try jogging, hiking staircases, or strengthening your legs through any continued cardiovascular exercise. Having a quality pack, broken in boots, and lightweight gear cannot be overrated when it comes to long western hikes. In fact, I feel boots and backpacks are the two most important pieces of western hunting gear. Whatever your preferred methods are, get your muscles into gear long before the season begins.

Prescribing the appropriate training regimen for all individuals is impossible, as different individuals will require different amounts of physical exercise to get in shape for a western hunt. Not all hunts are in the same type of terrain or weather either. Nevertheless, I will explain some general desired results to give a basic idea of a typical day in the field. At the conclusion of your training, a DIY western elk hunter should comfortably be able to hike five to fifteen miles each day, in rough off trail terrain, both ascending and descending elevation, through snow at depths of one foot or more. You should be able to do so while carrying your bow or rifle and a fifteen to twenty five pound pack. In addition, you must be physically able to responsibly pack out your game if you harvest an animal. You should continue to work out in the months prior to your hunt until you are comfortable with this type of hunting. Remember, you will likely be repeating this process multiple days in a row.

Hiking the Williams Fork Range, Colorado

Not all hunts are as physically demanding as others and you do not always encounter foul weather. Some western terrain is actually pretty mild, but don't count on it. Research where and how you will be hunting. Get a good idea of what the physical requirements will be. Try to replicate and prepare yourself for the exact type of hunt you will be embarking on. Being in better shape than required will certainly be rewarded. In western hunting, you typically end up going much further than you originally anticipated. If fatigue requires you to hunt hard on day one and take a break on day two, it is much better than not travelling far on either day. Keep in mind that many hunters do not travel very far from their vehicle and game tends to hang out in areas further away. Being physically fit and able to travel long distances will be put you in the game and away from the pressure. Even if the reward is not in the form of a kill, you will be very happy to avoid the aches and pains associated with over exhausting yourself.

Chapter 13 - Planning Summary

It's time to put all the pieces together. This reading began by illustrating what western hunting is and the terrain it takes place on. It asked the reader to be realistic and look internally to see what type of hunt is preferred. It explained the license game and introduced the resources needed to make educated decisions. An introduction to logistics, gear, and physical conditioning was also given. After soaking this information in, let's bring it all together.

Assume you are ready to start planning for an upcoming hunt. You recognize what the license game is and are determined to have realistic expectations on the hunt you choose to embark on. So where do you begin? Below is an overall western hunt planning summary.

Step 1: Creating a Plan

Ask yourself the Creating a Plan questions from Chapter 7. Think about what your objectives are in a western hunt. Resolve whether you should hire a guide or embark on a DIY hunt. Come to terms with the realities of western hunting and be prepared to manage your expectations based on your options. Consider the license game and the process of obtaining quality western tags. Decide what type of hunt you wish to pursue.

Step 2: Research Scouting for Tag Planning

Decide if you want to research tag data by yourself or subscribe to an application service magazine. Employ the tag planning research resources as described in Chapter 8 to the maximum extent of your ability. Compare your top choice units and decide on a tag.

Step 3: Apply for Tags

Enter the license game and apply for the units you researched in Step 2. Follow the application procedures of each respective state to send in your applications. Be sure to track your applications, unit preferences, and points as described in Chapter 7. Good luck in the draw!

Step 4: Research Scouting for Hunt Planning

Employ the hunt-planning research resources as described in Chapter 8 to the maximum extent of your ability. Locate your target hunting areas and compare them to one another. Choose your top locations and formulate a plan based on the knowledge you have gained.

Step 5: Preparation & Logistics

Now that you have your tag in hand and have chosen your hunting location it is time to put together all of the details that will make your hunt possible. This includes getting in shape, deciding on and booking your lodging, setting up transportation, and acquiring all your needed gear and supplies.

After you have completed the above five steps you are ready to go begin your hunting trip. Remember that the time and effort put into planning will have a direct effect on the success and level of comfort of your hunting trip. You will only get out what you put into the trip. Have fun and be safe, and as always, good luck!

Chapter 14 - The Hunt

With all of the advice offered in this guide, one may be asking what does it realistically look like when the plan comes together. For that, I will offer an example of a recent hunt wherein the suggestions in this book were put into practice. This particular hunt takes place in Colorado and I will summarize the process and results in this chapter.

Each year my oldest brother travels out West for an elk hunt. As our success has continued to increase over the years, my father, uncle, and other brother began to express interest in western hunting. The first of many trips was agreed to take place the following year. All hunters wished to pursue elk and mule deer. Over Thanksgiving in 2011 we discussed our options. As they had little to no experience in western hunting, I was to arrange the trip. A few items quickly came to mind during our discussions. With my father and uncle being over sixty years old, the hunt would need to be in somewhat mild terrain. My father also requested accommodations more hospitable than a camper or tent. With no experience elk hunting, they requested to hunt with a rifle rather than a primitive weapon. They also did not have any elk points built up in any states.

My permanent residence is in Colorado. Given the ability for me to scout and for them to obtain tags with no points built up, a Colorado hunt was the quick and easy choice. I was also already very familiar with the seasons, regulations, weather, etc., so I would not need to overly pursue the first resource, which is of course the Colorado state hunting regulations.

Initially I considered taking everyone to my usual hunting grounds. However, my favorite hunting area is very high in elevation and in very difficult terrain. Wilderness areas can be a tough hunt if you are not in great shape and I was also worried of the probability of my family getting lost. My usual hot spot simply would not work. I would need to take them to a more forgiving area. I was basically starting from square one as an outfitter with the whole state in my scope.

Preliminary discussions established a set of expectations for the trip. I discussed the reality of easy to obtain tags and let them know that if they wished to hunt both mule deer and elk it would require us to purchase OTC second season elk tags. High pressure tags are not a recommended type of DIY hunting. These tags have low success rates and hunting both types of game can be very difficult, as they do not always inhabit the same areas at the same time. Our overall conclusion was that this was to be the first of many hunts and that an OTC tag this year would ready them for better hunts in the future. They wished to get to know an area and familiarize themselves with western hunting. In this manner they could return with points for a better hunt in one of the following years. For the current year, my father, uncle, and middle brother would apply for buck deer tags and cow elk tags. My oldest brother and I would purchase OTC bull elk tags. I then set out to do some research.

Pre-hunt Photo, Colorado

The first resource I utilized was the Colorado Parks and Wildlife website. Usually I would recommend looking into the regulations first, but I am already very familiar with the Colorado regulations and seasons. I also belong to multiple

Application Service Magazines, but these services usually avoid recommending OTC units and tend to point out the best units in the state written from a nonresident perspective. Thus application service magazines would only point me to the more difficult to draw units in Colorado, something that was out of reach for the current year. My family was not expecting trophy class animals either; any mature animal would be a welcomed harvest. So I needed to complete all my tag research on my own. No problem, the Colorado parks and Wildlife statistics offered everything I needed.

Colorado is known for elk opportunity, a lot of elk and a lot of hunters. It is also known for great mule deer hunting, in both quality and opportunity, a trait that is difficult to find across the West these days. I needed to find an area with OTC elk tags and easy to draw mule deer tags. The area needed mild terrain, good success statistics, and close by hotel/motel accommodations. Most importantly, it needed to offer the possibility of a good future elk hunt, so that meant good success rates during the earlier draw seasons, those being muzzleloader or first rifle. It may sound like a steep order, but you would be surprised of the options available to Colorado hunters in all of those categories. With elk as the priority, finding a good elk tag was the first goal. Navigating the website, I printed out a colored map of all of the Colorado OTC elk units. The map showed the boundaries of all units within the state, with the OTC units colored orange. Colorado regularly publishes yearly hunting statistics and regional hunting guides. The regional hunting guides are printable brochures that break the state up into four quadrants. Each guide covers one quadrant or region (e.g. Northwest), and covers all units within that region of the state. The guide analyzes each unit by hunting season and provides terrain descriptions, success rates, and hunter pressure. In general, these guides take the raw data from the published statistics and organize it into easy to follow information. As you can imagine, this is an extremely useful tool for Colorado hunters. Colorado offers OTC elk tags for both the second and third rifle seasons. These are deer seasons as well. Common sense told me the second season

160

would be better for elk as the elk would be less pressured. A brief glance at a few unit success rates quickly confirmed this. Knowing I would target second season, I scrolled through the hunting guides looking at the first season rifle success rates. The long-term plan was to return in the future for a first season hunt, so first season success rates were the priority. While doing so, I jotted down the first season success rate for all OTC units, within that unit, on the map I had printed out. This took less than an hour. When all were written down on the map, I looked it over and highlighted the three highest success rate units.

My next investigation would compare the top two units. I would leave the third on the back burner if these two did not work out. The elk success rates in these units had a respective five-year first season average of 51% and 44%, pretty good. I also looked at the second season success rate to ensure consistency. Both were at about half of the first season. Hard to imagine the difference one week makes, I guess that proves how much elk react to hunter pressure. I then looked over the deer success rate statistics and found the five year average at 22% and 34% for the second season. This is the first rifle season you may hunt deer in Colorado even though it is the second rifle season for elk. A deer season success rate at 22% is just below average when comparing it to other units, but that was acceptable for this hunt as deer were our second priority. So I had the highest first rifle season OTC elk unit, even though we would be hunting second season, and an average deer unit in hand. Next I looked at the hunting pressure. The pressure was about 400 hunters in both units. Given the size of the units, this didn't seem very bad. Units vary in size, and some comparably sized units had more than 1,000 hunters. Others had less than 400, but in comparison to some of my next in line choices this seemed about average. So far, both units looked pretty good. One had slightly better elk rates and the other had slightly better deer rates. Both had comparable pressure to other units with high success rates.

Next I pulled up Google maps to look over the terrain and check for ample public land. Colorado is littered with very difficult terrain and public land tends to fall on difficult terrain. I was looking for enough land to scout and hunt multiple areas and also to spread hunters out a bit. A quick glance revealed that my first choice unit had slightly more National Forest land than my second. Looking at additional maps, neither unit contained BLM land. Both units had a few small tracts of state land. Both units had enough public land for a good hunt, but the majority of the land in each unit was private. This can be seen as both positive and negative. Sometimes success rates can be skewed higher by private land. On the other hand, some hunters target hunting areas that border private land for spillover effects. Given that the units still had considerable public land, I chose to move forward. Next I looked over the terrain to see if my father and uncle would be comfortable hunting there. I was very fortunate that both of these units had a good range of mild to difficult terrain. This would keep them happy and hunting for multiple days, with the option of strenuous terrain if desired. Fatigue can ruin a hunt; both units looked suitable for multi-day hunting.

My final unit requirement to consider was accommodations. My father had requested we rent some type of lodging rather than camp. This proved to be the deal breaker for my number one unit. It had no suitable lodging accommodations within forty-five minutes of the public land. Hunters will often find themselves making compromises with hunting trip objectives. Our dilemma was a common one. Should we choose to rough it and camp with better odds of hunter success or should we choose comfort with lower odds of success? The youthful choice is usually to rough it, but the latter choice prevailed. Hunters need to make realistic choices. By choosing the second choice unit, we decreased our success rate for elk by 7%. However we increased our deer success rate by 12%. We also ensured that our hunting group would be in better spirits. But our expectations would need to reflect our choice. By accepting comfort as our preference, we had sacrificed our odds of success, plain and simple. However the sacrifice was quite small given the second choice unit still looked pretty good.

Now that I had completed the tag-planning phase of research scouting, it was time to send in our applications. I assisted my family members with their online applications regarding submission dates, unit codes, and miscellaneous application questions. I also ensured they put in for elk points so we could draw this unit for a future hunt in a preferred season. In Colorado you can build preference points and purchase OTC tags in the same year. You can also build points with your first application choice and draw your second; this comes in very handy if you want a cow tag. I even convinced my brothers and father to apply for points in a few other states as well. Jumping ahead a few months, everyone drew their deer and elk tags. We knew these tags were guaranteed to be drawn by researching the draw success rates in the Colorado state wildlife statistics. In tag planning, we had only researched units that we know we would draw. My oldest brother and I then purchased our bull tags over the counter. With tags in hand, it was time for me to do some hunt planning.

When planning a hunt, I always begin by pouring over maps again and again. Many hunting retail locations across the West sell maps of designated hunting units. I quickly purchased one of our unit and began to examine this map. I alternated looking over the map and looking over Google maps and Google earth for an interactive view. We would be hunting in mid-October. Feeding would primarily drive elk behavior. We would be lucky to catch any rutting activity. Migratory movements would yet to begin. This was the second rifle season. The first season was to take place the week before we arrived and would last five days. This gave the game two days of rest before my season began. It was safe to say that the elk would be pressured, but not in the extreme sense. I was searching for areas moderately pressured elk would be feeding and bedding. This meant searching for open feeding areas with adjacent bedding areas well off the beaten path.

The elk would be away from hunter access areas and dependent upon heavily timbered hideouts. On my hard copy map, I located and circled eight places that looked like potential feeding areas. These were open parks or aspen groves more than a mile from any public access. Knowing this was an OTC hunt, I tried to use logical methods to avoid hunter pressure. For instance, when circling my potential hunting spots, I avoided public land areas with multiple roads crisscrossing the land. Areas that have a lot of roads attract road hunters and as a basic rule of thumb, the better the public access the more of the public you will see. I located one area that was day use only with no overnight parking or camping. This type of area minimizes hunting because many non-resident hunters prefer to hunt right from camp. Thus they simply avoid hunting areas where they cannot camp. I located another area that required a hunter to access it only by crossing or walking around a sizable lake. Most hunters will simply overlook an area that has a large barrier in the way. Two areas I located required a hunter to leave the parking area and walk the edge of private land for over a mile before turning into the large mass of public land. This method would get me out of the main valley accessed by the parking area. The rest of the areas I located required an extensive walk to reach. Going further back usually separates you from quite a few hunters. You can never expect absolute solitude, but the further you go the less pressure you will find. All of the areas I located appeared to have the characteristics of feeding areas (open terrain or aspen breaks) with bedding areas close by (heavily timbered steep North and East facing slopes). In addition, all had some reasonable method of avoiding hunter pressure.

Next I would attempt to confirm some of my research through online searches for websites, forums, and blogs. I quickly found that my unit was not a popular discussion online. From one perspective, this can be good news as it indicates it is not extremely pressured. However, it may also indicate that it may not be overly popular due it being not that great of hunting. Nevertheless, the statistics supported its worth so I endeared to pursue other means of research. The one valuable piece of information I gleamed from online searches was that sometimes the forest service allows local sheep and cattle farms to graze in the unit. This information would come in handy when scouting, as cattle signs can sometimes be

164

confusing with elk sign. Also, goat-herding pressure can sometimes push elk. So if possible, I would try to avoid areas where goats were grazing.

My next line of research was to contact state and federal employees with direct experience working in my unit. If at all possible, I attempt to do so in person. Due to simple logistics, many hunters do this via telephone. I was planning a scouting trip to the unit over the summer. I looked up the addresses of the local Colorado Parks and Wildlife office, the local Forest Service office, and a nearby state park. I would visit all locations during my trip and ask as many questions as I could. Another resource is any hunter with previous experience in the unit. As this resource is somewhat harder to plan for, I hoped I could meet someone while in the unit that may offer some information.

As spring warmed into the summer, I began to put together a scouting trip. I had a few days off over the fourth of July, and decided this would be a great opportunity to head up and do some scouting. The unit was about three and half hours from my home and I had never been there. I did read that a few local lakes and rivers had decent fishing, so a four day camping, scouting, and fishing trip was in the works. As I entered the unit, my first stop was the local Colorado Parks and Wildlife Office, which happened to be a joint office with the local Forest Service. I went to the main service desk and began my conversation by expressing my jealousy for the Wildlife Official's job. I then explained that I was headed onto the nearby National Forest for scouting and fishing. The first employee quickly called over a more knowledgeable Forest Service employee to help with recommendations. I asked of game movements, hunting pressure, and preferred areas. As I had guessed, pressure was concentrated around the larger camping areas. Game movements were also typical. Elk and deer remained high in the summer, moving downward with the rut, and down even further with pressure and weather. General movements were westward, which of course was down in elevation. West also led to mostly private land. They recommended a few regions in general, one of which being the lake area I had denoted. I then spread out my map with my targeted areas circled and showed them where I was planning to scout. They quickly confirmed a couple of the other areas I had circled as being worthwhile. With many thanks, I headed off to the state park, which happened to be very close to the area where I planned to do the bulk of my scouting. I commenced my discussions with the state park officials in the same manner as I had with the Wildlife and Forest Service Office. I have always had pleasant experiences with state and federal personnel, possibly because they often share a love for the sport of hunting. Recommendations of game movements, hunter pressure, and hunting areas to scout were once again given. Two seemed to be recurring in my discussions. One was the lake area and the other was the day use area I had located. I decided that these would be the first two areas I would scout. I then headed down to the state park lake for some trout fishing in the last few evening hours.

As I unloaded my fishing rods, a different State Park Official rode up on a bicycle and requested my fishing license. I happily furnished it and asked if he had any recommended hunting areas. He also noted the lake area as a prime hunting location. It was actually a different lake than the one I was fishing at. In addition, he even advised that I focus my fishing efforts in a few other areas. I casted a few lines anyway and soon headed off to a close by forest service access point to pitch camp for the weekend. To my dismay, the first forest service road I took led to a beautiful mountain meadow that was already occupied by a family of campers. Before turning around to head to a more secluded spot, I stepped out of my truck and asked the campers if they ever did any hunting in the area. To no surprise, the answer was yes. As mentioned in Chapter 8, this is the type of random "previous hunter" occurrence that can turn our to be quite beneficial. However, the hunters did not seem very fond of answering any questions related to specific recommended hunting areas. Quickly noticing this, I turned my attention to hunter pressure and they advised that the area we were currently in attracted a bulk of hunters as it had many access roads. I had previously guessed this was the case from my map research and I had only designated this as a camping area rather than a hunting area. Nonetheless, the confirmation of this was valuable.

Recollecting the information I had gained over the course of the day, I headed down the trail and found a suitable place to make camp. Over the next few days I ran into one more Forest Service employee who recommended the day use area and another area I had yet to identify. I also stopped into a local general store, which happened to be owned by a hunting outfitter. While purchasing a better map and some other supplies the outfitter and I discussed his offered services, the general hunting in the region, and the general areas he outfits in. One should recognize the privacy of hunting areas and be courteous of hunters and outfitters. Unlike state and federal employees, these individuals are providing personal information, so be respectful. Out of respect for outfitters, I usually do not even ask specific hunting location questions. However if they wish to mention some on their own, I am very pleased to listen. A few days into the trip I also helped a local rancher pull a log off the road with my truck. Upon inquiry, he confirmed an area I was heading into had plenty of game. Over the four days I was in my hunting unit, I gathered extensive information and hunting recommendations without even stepping foot into the woods to scout. I gathered that my top areas to scout would be behind the lake, the day use area, and an area next to some private ground. All of these areas I had looked at before entering my unit and all of which had been confirmed as hot spots by local officials.

Before I begin scouting on foot, I always like to drive all around my unit to get a good feel for the terrain and landscape. I had covered a good bit of ground the day I had arrived, but the following morning I went for a long ride. I knew the general areas I wished to scout, so I drove all around them through many available access roads. This gives you a better idea of vegetation, geographical features, escape routes, public land access, and road conditions. Some areas always inevitably look better than others. Areas you had only viewed on maps take actual form. I confirmed that my top three scouting locations looked very appealing, with the lake area and the day use area looking the best.

All my research thus far had led up to this point. All of my efforts had been to continuously whittle down my hunting location choices. I began with the whole state in mind, and now I was down to three recommended hunting areas within a specific unit. I headed to the lake location first as it looked great on the map and from the truck. I had been told it held plenty of game and had little to no pressure. I also knew it would be hard to get to. I quickly realized that this last characteristic would prove its downfall. My first attempt to access the area was from a nearby forest service road that would get me within a mile of the feeding and bedding area I had been recommended. Several miles from the spot I wished to park the road was closed to all vehicle traffic and securely locked. The road beyond the locked gate had not been maintained for some time and was completely overgrown. As I wasn't even remotely close, I moved to a different access point. This method was to access the area from a hiking trail that widely skirted the lake. Unfortunately the trail skirted too wide, was several miles too long for a feasible access route, and placed me too high above my target area. With a half day already lost, I tried another method for accessing it. This route tightly followed the lakeshore around and gained access with about an hour and a half of hiking. The route also seemed like it would be a bit tricky in snow and ice. I reasoned that a quick kayak trip would take me where I needed to be in about fifteen minutes, but this wouldn't be very helpful for five of us. Thus a tricky one and a half hour hike around a lake was the only access to the area. I started to realize why no one hunted there and also that it might prove too tricky to hunt with a group. My actual scouting that evening revealed a great feeding area, an adjacent bedding area, and multiple forms of heavy sign throughout the area. I found great trails, including a heavily used saddle, but my final determination was that this spot wouldn't be my top choice as getting there would simply be too difficult. I decided to focus on my second choice area the next day.

Day three of my trip would be comprised of a morning fishing trip and an evening scouting trip to the day use area. After some fishing success, I found my way to the day use area that afternoon. The road in was seemingly private, the parking area was quite small, and it was clearly marked as a day use area only. All of these items ensure a bit more privacy than typical trailheads. I try to scout hunting areas in the manner in which I hunt, and this day would provide for daytime still hunting and evening glassing. I wasn't as worried about pushing game, as I was still months away from the season. I made my way deep into the forest and quickly located heavy elk sign. It wasn't very long until I was seeing both elk and deer moving to feeding areas. I was instantly sold. I made my way to a few areas I had located on the map. I found heavy tracks, rubs, droppings, aspen scrapes, and even some cropped grassy areas on the way. I targeted open feeding areas and what looked to be travel routes on the map. The best sign is animals themselves, and in glassing sessions I saw elk and deer feeding. My family had little experience navigating long distance hikes through the mountains. Knowing this, I build a few ground blinds areas that my family could sit at while glassing. As the light faded, I reluctantly decided it was time to head back. On the hike out, I even encountered a decent bull. With all the sign and game sightings, I was already formulating hunting strategies. When you find a good hunting area, there is little question involved. You just know it. The day use area proved to be the best spot I scouted. I only hoped the pressure would be light during the hunting season.

The last day would take me to a new area altogether. Early in the morning I drove to an out of the way forest road that only went a few hundred yards into the National Forest before it was gaited and locked. On the hike in I paralleled private ground for a mile or so before dropping into a valley that would certainly be overlooked by most hunters. Hunting public land that closely borders private can have spillover benefits. However this area was somewhat lower in elevation than where I predicted the game to be during my hunting season. As I stalked the woods I located two feeding areas that looked surprisingly good, both of which I had not located on the map. Scouting always reveals information that simply cannot be found with maps. This was a classic example. I seemed to be locating more deer than elk sign. The area was also very thick. I spooked some game and found some good sign, but the area simply did not compare to the day use area. I decided that this would be a good back up hunting spot, but my main efforts would be at the day use area.

During my trip I also took a couple hikes from my camping location. This was mostly out of convenience, but also for the sheer love of scouting and the outdoors. It is always fun to see game and to cover new terrain. The area looked decent, but if you are told a spot will be pressured, its usually is. Game may be present throughout the summer, but hunter pressure will change game movements very quickly in spots that are simply too easy to access. My main focus would still be the day use area.

Over four days I had spoken with multiple individuals with first hand experience with the terrain and game in the area. I had focused my scouting on three main areas that looked great on the map and that had also been confirmed by local officials and hunters. I found considerable sign and saw a lot of game. I decided on my primary hunting location and also had a few back up spots. My hunting plan had come together, and I would target the day use area. Within that area I had multiple locations targeted as feeding and bedding areas and had a few strategies in mind as to how to hunt them.

Now that I had my hunting specifics lined up, I spent some time on logistics planning. While in the unit scouting hunting locations, I also looked at a few cabin rental options. Upon returning home and to an Internet source, I compared other hotel/motel rental options in the area. I ended up booking a two-bedroom cabin that I had looked at. Before doing so, I confirmed that it had the correct number of beds, blankets, cooking tools, and other miscellaneous supplies. Given the cooking options, I decided we would simply buy groceries in the nearest town upon arriving in the unit for our hunt. We would make breakfast and dinner in our cabin each day. Lunches would be packed, as we would be hunting full days. With lodging and sustenance accounted for, I looked to our transportation needs. Our lodging was about fifteen minutes from the day use area that we planned to hunt. Five hunters would have different plans, success, and fatigue. We would need two vehicles to accommodate our differing needs, all of our gear, and any trips for supplies or to butcher shops. In addition to my truck, we would need to rent a vehicle. Luckily a friend agreed to lend me his truck while I rented him an economy class vehicle for the week. I also looked up local butcher shops, prices, and hours of operation. I then looked into a few meat-shipping options. These included services from butcher shops, commercial shipping companies, and coolers to be taken on planes. Given the cost of shipping, my family decided that they would rent a vehicle and drive home rather than fly. Interestingly enough, it made more economical sense to fly to Colorado and drive home with any meat and antlers taken. This was certainly a gamble, as deciding beforehand to drive home would not have made much sense if there were no meat to carry. But as with most hunts, hopes were high. After decisions were made and bookings were complete, I sent a long detailed email to my family. The email included hunting plans, costs, logistics, physical training requirements, and recommended gear. The physical training and gear recommendations returned replies of "is that really necessary?" But my family reluctantly agreed and over the next few months I had multiple calls discussing gear, the hunt itself, and physical training. With lodging, transportation, and sustenance planned for, just about all my hunt planning was complete. There was little more to do than wait for opening day. Given work restraints, we would not be able to show up to the unit any more than one day in advance of the season for some quick scouting.

All hunting trips should account for time before the hunt to acclimate, gather provisions, and sight in guns. My family arrived in Denver Thursday afternoon before the opener on Saturday. Over the next day and a half we sighted in weapons, travelled to our hunting area, bought groceries, checked into our cabin, and readied our gear. We also went on a scouting trip to the day use area. I dispersed maps with ground blinds, glassing areas, and target hunting areas identified. As we hiked in, I pointed out many of our target hunting locations from a distance. We even watched a group of elk that evening feed down through the main drainage in the valley. The next day, it was time to go hunting.

The previous paragraphs describe all the suggestions of this book put into practice. Our hunting unit was not known for Boone and Crockett game and you won't read about it in any hunting magazines. We had three buck tags, three cow tags, and two bull tags. Of our hunting group, two of us had experience hunting the West and three had none. I was the only person who had thoroughly scouted the unit. Nevertheless, I had completed all the planning needed for a successful hunt and had advised as to the proper expectations.

Our hunt turned out to be very successful. Over the course of seven days, we took two cows and one bull. In addition, I knocked a bull down that didn't stay down. While unfortunate, that is a reality of hunting sometimes. The deer seemed to have vacated the area before our arrival. Only two shooter bucks were seen, and the hunters without deer tags saw them both. Interestingly enough, we actually ran into the local outfitter I had spoken to as he was guiding on horseback in our area. The day use area was not a location he had disclosed to me the previous summer, but it was a definite indication that we were in a good area. He also confirmed that deer were very prevalent in the area until about a week before our season began. They must have decided to migrate to lower elevations early that year. Once again, this is a reality of western hunting. Sometimes the game moves out of areas completely. Even so, we had taken three elk with five elk tags. That is a 60% success rate on a hunt with a 23% average; that's twice the average! Not to mention the additional sighting opportunities and the bull that got away.

Our hunt turned out to be just what we wanted, and more than we expected. It is a realistic description of what a western hunt can be if you perform the right planning. We had great opportunities and great success. We didn't harvest any deer, but elk were our prime target. In addition, we learned the game habits and became very familiar with the terrain for a future hunt. I actually returned the following bow season and arrowed a very nice bull. Our plan is to return in another year or so for an early season muzzleloader hunt. Now that my family knows the unit, they will be much more successful in the future when they return. Given we had little to no experience in the unit before our hunt, much of the success can be attributed to the extensive tag and hunt planning performed in the months leading up to the hunt. When planning a hunt, don't take research lightly; it is the most important aspect of western hunting. Do your research and plan accordingly!

Chapter 15 – Why We Hunt

Some say leaders are born and not raised, I say the same for hunters. Call it a primal instinct we have from birth. What drives wolves to hunt? If only necessity, why do domestic dogs stalk rabbits, squirrels, and deer? It's instinctive, but they also enjoy it. Humans hunted out of necessity for centuries. It's instinctive for us. Now we do it by choice, because we enjoy it too. It's in our blood. It's the natural order of our ecosystem and food chain. Humans eat meat. The natural method to obtain meat is to hunt for it.

When asked what drives us to hunt, hunters sometimes have difficulty. We have difficulty because we are attempting to describe instinct. We feel compelled to hunt. We feel compelled to spend time outdoors and to witness the natural life of this planet. We enjoy matching our wits against the game. The problem solving, the chase, the thrill, the chance, they all drive us. We desire the inner compulsion and passion driven by instinct.

Nonetheless, there is a definite distinction between humans and animals. We have God given intelligence, and with it power and dominion over the animals and wilderness. Along with it comes the responsibility to appropriately manage and sustain our great outdoors. That sustainability has been strongly supported by the contributions of contemporary hunters, mostly through financial and legal support through the purchase of hunting and fishing licenses. That gives all hunters something to be proud of.

Todd C. Wilson, Author

Sources

i US Forest Service. (12/22/2009). *About Us – Meet the Forest Service.* Retrieved 10/15/2013 from http://www.fs.fed.us/aboutus/meetfs.shtml.

ii US Department of the Interior Bureau of Land Management. (1/26/2012). *The Bureau of Land Management: Who We Are, What We Do.* Retrieved 10/15/2013 from http://www.blm.gov/wo/st/en/info/About_BLM.html.

iiiColorado Parks and Wildlife. (8/2013). *Big Game Hunting Quick Guide.* Retrieved 11/18/2013 from http://wildlife.state.co.us/SiteCollectionDocuments/DOW/Hunting/BigGame/BigGameHuntingQuickGuide.pdf.

iv Maryland Department of Natural Resources. *White-tailed Deer (Odocoileus virginianus) Description and Range.* Retrieved 11/16/13 from http://www.dnr.state.md.us/wildlife/Hunt_Trap/deer/wtdeerbiology.asp.

v United States Department of Agriculture, Natural Resource Conservation Service. (November 1999). American Elk (Cervus elaphus). *Fish and Wildlife Habitat Management Leaflet, Number 11.* Retrieved 11/15/13 from http://www.sciencebuddies.org/science-fair-projects/project_apa_format_examples.shtml.

vi 1995-2013 Healthwise, Incorporated. (March 29, 2011). Altitude Sickness, Topic Overview. Retrieved 11/11/13 from http://www.webmd.com/a-to-z-guides/altitude-sickness-topic-overview.

Made in the USA
Middletown, DE
10 March 2017